Incentive Early Retirement Programs for Faculty:
Innovative Responses to a Changing Environment

by Jay L. Chronister and Thomas R. Kepple, Jr.

ASHE-ERIC Higher Education Report No. 1, 1987

Prepared by

Clearinghouse on Higher Education
The George Washington University

Published by

Jonathan D. Fife,
Series Editor

Association for the Study of Higher
Education

Cite as
Chronister, Jay L., and Kepple, Thomas R., Jr. *Incentive Early Retirement Programs for Faculty: Innovative Responses to a Changing Environment*. ASHE-ERIC Higher Education Report No. 1. Washington, D.C.: Association for the Study of Higher Education, 1987.

Managing Editor: Christopher Rigaux

The ERIC Clearinghouse on Higher Education invites individuals to submit proposals for writing monographs for the Higher Education Report series. Proposals must include:
1. A detailed manuscript proposal of not more than five pages.
2. A chapter-by-chapter outline.
3. A 75-word summary to be used by several review committees for the initial screening and rating of each proposal.
4. A vita.
5. A writing sample.

Library of Congress Catalog Card Number 87-70886
ISSN 0884-0040
ISBN 0-913317-36-5

Cover design by Michael David Brown, Rockville, Maryland.

ERIC **Clearinghouse on Higher Education**
The George Washington University
One Dupont Circle, Suite 630
Washington, D.C. 20036

ASHE **Association for the Study of Higher Education**
One Dupont Circle, Suite 630
Washington, D.C. 20036

*Office of Educational
Research and Improvement
U.S. Department of Education*

This publication was prepared partially with funding from the Office of Educational Research and Improvement, U.S. Department of Education, under contract no. 400-86-0017. The opinions expressed in this report do not necessarily reflect the positions or policies of OERI or the Department.

EXECUTIVE SUMMARY

Incentive early retirement programs designed to encourage and facilitate the retirement of faculty before mandatory or a regular retirement age have become increasingly popular on college campuses during the past decade.

This monograph provides an extensive review of the literature on incentive early retirement programs, including the findings of several studies designed to assess the effectiveness of such programs. It addresses several topics: the reasons for which institutions develop the programs, key concepts and terms relevant to the topic, characteristics of different types of programs and the incentives offered, legal issues that must be addressed, costs and benefits, strategies for assessing the feasibility of developing programs, and an assessment of the success of programs.

What Are Incentive Early Retirement Programs?

Incentive early retirement programs are an arrangement between an employer and an employee that provides a tangible inducement or reward for early retirement. The decision is voluntary on the part of the employee, and the incentives are structured so that within institutionally established criteria, the faculty member identifies himself or herself as a candidate for participation.

Such programs may be ad hoc in nature—in which the faculty member individually negotiates the incentives (benefits) with the institution—or formal—in which the institution has established the incentives that will be offered to a class of faculty identified as meeting the institution's criteria for eligibility to participate.

These programs can be classified as benefiting primarily faculty or the institution, depending upon the reasons for which they are established. A recent study of programs in 51 public institutions identified nearly 60 percent of the incentive offerings as being beneficial to the institution (Chronister and Trainer 1985a).

The most common incentives used in early retirement programs include a severance-pay or lump-sum payment, a liberalized actuarial reduction, annuity enhancements, bridging benefit payments, partial or phased retirement, and/or other basically nonmonetary perquisites. Most institutional programs include combinations of incentives to meet the diverse interests of faculty. A study of 39 private liberal arts colleges found that nearly 21 percent of the institutions offered two or more incentive options to faculty (Kepple 1984), while among the 51 public universities, approximately 55 percent of the institutions offered multiple incentives (Chronister and Trainer 1985a).

How Are Programs Developed?

Assessing the feasibility of establishing an incentive early retirement program is a complex undertaking. The development of such a program must be based on the characteristics of an institution's basic retirement plan, the needs the program is designed to address, and the relevant characteristics of the faculty to whom it is addressed. Whether an institution has a defined contribution or a defined benefit retirement plan has important implications for the nature of the incentives that might be required.

A key question that will affect the nature and success of an early retirement program relates to the role of the faculty in its development. Most early retirement programs identified as successful in this report involved faculty committees or representation in program development. Such involvement ensures that faculty concerns are addressed during development of the program and provides for faculty members' better understanding of the purposes for which the program is created.

The age distribution of faculty and their historical retirement patterns have implications for choosing the threshold age for faculty participation. Activities important to developing an incentive program include computer flow modeling of faculty on selected characteristics, such as age and tenure status, under differing assumptions and cost/benefit analysis of different incentive options from both the institution's and the faculty's perspectives.

A number of federal and state statutes and regulations must be considered in program development. Incentive early retirement programs may be affected by the current social security law, the Employee Retirement Income Security Act, the Age Discrimination in Employment Act as amended in 1978 and 1986, and federal tax considerations, including those introduced by the Tax Reform Act of 1986. Federal statutes and regulations in particular often present complex legal problems, and the implications for the institution and the individual may be far from inconsequential. Moreover, certain state statutes may also be applicable. It is therefore important that legal counsel be involved in the process at some time before the program is implemented.

Have Early Retirement Programs Been Successful?
Although observers do not agree unanimously on the effectiveness of incentive early retirement programs, the majority of the information gathered for this report supports the use of the programs. This observation is not intended to present such programs as a panacea for curing staffing problems or financial woes, however.

In assessing the effectiveness and success of these incentive programs, it is necessary to view them from the perspectives of both institutions and faculty participants. Success from the institutional view may be a function of such factors as the number of vacancies created, a reduction in tenure ratio, and/or a reduction in personnel costs. Success from the faculty's perspective can be assessed in terms of whether the program allows the individual to pursue personal and professional objectives that continued employment would deter and whether the retiree's income after retirement permits the maintenance of a lifestyle that is approximately equivalent to that of retiring at a "normal" age. The degree to which eligible faculty members actually participate in the program may be viewed as a measure of a program's success.

Nearly 49 percent of the 39 liberal arts colleges cited in this monograph indicated that faculty participation in their early retirement programs equaled or exceeded expectations, while 42 percent stated their programs had not been in existence long enough to make a judgment (Kepple 1984). Although no explicit numerical goals had been established for the majority of programs at the 51 public universities, 80 percent of the institutions offering full early retirement options indicated that faculty participation had been at or above the expected level (Chronister and Trainer 1985a).

The limited number of published studies about faculty reactions to participation in incentive early retirement programs indicates generally positive acceptance. A 1977 study of early retirees found that 93 percent of the early retirees were satisfied with their decision and 90 percent would make the same decision again (Patton 1979).

The use of formal incentive programs can also significantly affect the quality of a campus. A number of institutions have reported that as a result of offering an attractive incentive retirement program, they lost senior faculty members that they would rather not have lost.

What Is the Future of Incentive Early Retirement Programs? Incentive early retirement programs have been generally termed successful in meeting the purposes for which they were established at most campuses. With passage of the amendments to the Age Discrimination in Employment Act, which abolished mandatory retirement by reason of age, and with the growth in the proportion of the faculty who will be 55 to 65 over the next 15 years, incentive early retirement programs should become increasingly popular as a personnel management tool, recognizing that to be effective such programs must address the interests and needs of faculty.

ADVISORY BOARD

CONSULTING EDITORS

Paul A. Albrecht
Executive Vice President and Dean
Claremont Graduate School

G. Lester Anderson
Professor Emeritus
Pennsylvania State University

Robert C. Andringa
President
Creative Solutions

Carole J. Bland
Associate Professor, Family Practice and Community
  Health
University of Minnesota

L. Leon Campbell
Provost and Vice President for Academic Affairs
University of Delaware

Judith A. Clementson-Mohr
Director of Psychological Services
Purdue University

Mark H. Curtis
President Emeritus
Association of American Colleges

Roderick S. French
Vice President for Academic Affairs
George Washington University

Timothy Gallineau
Vice President for Student Development
Saint Bonaventure University

Milton Greenberg
Provost
American University

James C. Hearn
Associate Professor, Educational Policy and
  Administration
University of Minnesota

Margaret Heim
Senior Research Officer
Teachers Insurance and Annuity Association/
College Retirement Equity Fund

Hans H. Jenny
Executive Vice President
Chapman College

CONTENTS

FOREWORD

For the past several years, the issue of the aging professoriate has been recognized as one of the most critical problems facing higher education today. This topic was addressed most eloquently by Christine M. Licata in the recent 1986 ASHE-ERIC Higher Education Report, *Post-tenure Faculty Evaluation: Threat or Opportunity?* Effective incentive early retirement programs, like post-tenure evaluation plans, should be linked with faculty development. The amendment to the Age Discrimination in Employment Act, passed in 1986 with a potential effective date for higher education of 1994, makes this issue even more important. Basically this amendment says that age is no longer an acceptable criterion for forced retirement, and has heightened concern about elderly faculty.

The concept of reviewing faculty after tenure—either for development and renewal or for performance—is still controversial. Because it is controversial, many faculty and administrators find the issue unappetizing and would rather seek a solution through early retirement.

There are many reasons why early retirement programs are more appealing. First and foremost, on the surface these programs appear to be a 'win-win' situation. The institution wins in the long run by reducing salary expenditures and opening new faculty positions for either reassignment or replacement with younger faculty. The faculty wins since these programs are voluntary and only those who wish need take advantage of this opportunity.

In reality, early retirement programs are more complicated. Unless carefully devised, they can have more losers than winners. Not only should the legal and tax considerations be carefully reviewed by counsel, but a careful examination of which faculty might be tempted to take advantage of the opportunity is also advised. Another consideration is who will fill the insurance gap between early retirement and the minimum age for Medicare and Medicaid. There is a delicate line also to be drawn between offering incentives only to a targeted faculty—which can be construed as discriminatory—and yet not losing all the best faculty either.

In this monograph, Jay Chronister, professor and associate dean of the University of Virginia, and Thomas Kepple, Jr., provost of Rhodes College, give a succinct review of the literature and a careful study of institutional experi-

---

ences with such programs. The caveats contained in the conclusions and recommendations section provide vital guidance in even considering the feasibility of starting such a program.

As presidents, chief executive officers, branch presidents, and other administrators and faculty consider initiating early retirement programs, this monograph will be an invaluable aid. Early retirement programs are complex, difficult, and deceptive, yet all the more vital due to recent legislation and the expectation of more such legislation. The issues of fairness, academic freedom, vitality, and accountability are inextricably woven together here. This report will help make the long-term decisions more rational.

Jonathan D. Fife
Series Editor
Professor and Director
ERIC Clearinghouse on Higher Education
The George Washington University

ACKNOWLEDGMENTS

The completion of the research that supported the preparation of this report required the cooperation and collaboration of many individuals. The authors are indebted to the many institutional representatives who responded to the survey instruments and telephone interviews that formed the basis of their separate research in recent years.

Three individuals associated with the Center for the Study of Higher Education at the University of Virginia contributed to the project. Aileen Trainer was involved in the 1984 study of early retirement programs at 51 public institutions that is cited in this report. She was responsible for gathering and analyzing the data in that study. Bonnie Clevenger was responsible for gathering data, conducting telephone interviews, and developing the case studies of early retirement programs at three institutions in 1985 and 1986. Michael Ostroski has been conducting library research, so critical to the completion of a venture such as this one.

Special thanks are due to Rebecca Shifflett and Candace Chronister, who assisted in the typing of the manuscript.

INTRODUCTION

Contemporary higher education faces many critical issues brought about by changing social, political, demographic, and economic conditions. Faculty staffing, a particularly acute problem, has been the subject of significant research and institutional policy development in recent years. Stable or declining enrollments, financial constraints, students' changing interests, the characteristics of the professoriate itself, recent legislation uncapping the mandatory retirement age—all have combined to affect the flexibility that institutions deem necessary to meet current and future curricular and financial needs.

The literature on higher education suffers no dearth of information on the needs of colleges and universities for change in the composition of faculties during a time of management's constrained flexibility (see, for example, Bowen and Schuster 1986; Chronister 1984; Mortimer, Bagshaw, and Caruso 1985; Mortimer, Bagshaw, and Masland 1985; Patton 1979). Institutions have explored a variety of management strategies for creating an increased rate of turnover of faculty positions to provide for a continuing influx of new faculty, to respond to students' changing programmatic interests, to continue initiatives in the hiring of women and minorities, to reduce tenure ratios, to increase academic quality, or to reduce staff in the face of financial constraints. Their primary purpose has been to create a turnover in faculty positions that will exceed the turnover provided by historical rates of faculty retirements and other involuntary and voluntary separations.

Recent studies indicate that incentive early retirement programs for faculty are one approach that colleges and universities are using to deal with staffing problems (Chronister and Trainer 1985a; Kepple 1984; Mortimer, Bagshaw, and Masland 1985; Patton 1979). Such programs are management strategies designed to facilitate turnover in faculty positions in support of one or more institutional purposes or objectives.

This report reviews extensively the literature on incentive early retirement programs as well as findings and observations from case studies of a number of institutions that have such programs. Topics addressed include factors that institutions cite as serving as the impetus for developing the programs, characteristics of different types of programs, legal considerations and requirements that must be recognized and accommodated in the development of programs, institutional and individual cost/benefit considerations, strategies for assessing the feasibility of program development, and an assessment of the advantages and disadvantages of early retirement programs from both institutional and faculty perspectives.

The report includes five major sections. The first section briefly reviews environmental factors that have been described as creating the milieu in which early retirement programs have developed. The second section discusses different types of programs and the purposes for which they have been established, as well as definitions and an elaboration of the key concepts and terminology necessary to understand the topic. The third section presents strategies and factors to be considered in deciding upon the development of programs, using material from case studies. The fourth section presents the experiences of selected institutions that have implemented early retirement programs and the reactions of faculty to such programs. The final section presents conclusions and recommendations for institutions considering the establishment or revision of incentive early retirement programs.

THE ENVIRONMENT OF HIGHER EDUCATION

The environment in which institutions of higher education find themselves in the mid-1980s is well described in the phrase "uncertainty in the face of scarce resources" (Mortimer, Bagshaw, and Masland 1985, p. 5). The problems of uncertainty in student enrollments created by the decline in the size of the traditional college-age population, the pressure for increased institutionally funded financial aid, the volatility of federal support, the need to replace and upgrade computer equipment, scientific equipment, and facilities in general, the residual effects of inflation on institutional operations, and the problematic nature of state support for higher education in recent years are generally accepted as having significant implications for the continued vitality of colleges and universities.

The number of full-time residential faculty in colleges and universities [has grown] from about 154,000 in 1960 to approximately . . . 466,000 [by 1980].

But colleges and universities must also address several other important factors directly related to faculty staffing: the increased costs of faculty compensation, shifts in students' course preferences, the demographic characteristics of the professoriate itself, a general malaise among faculty that has become increasingly evident in recent years, and the influence of the amendments to the Age Discrimination in Employment Act (ADEA). These factors, although not applicable to all institutions to the same degree, deserve amplification because of their relationship to issues of faculty staffing in general and to questions of flexibility in particular.

Growth in the Number of Faculty
The exponential growth of higher education in this country from the late 1950s through the early 1970s led to a growth in the number of full-time residential faculty in colleges and universities from about 154,000 in 1960 to approximately 369,000 in 1970 (National Center for Education Statistics 1979, p. 104). By 1980, the full-time instructional faculty was estimated to have reached 466,000 (American Council on Education 1984, p. 114). As a result of that significant growth over the past two decades, higher education entered the 1980s with a relatively young professoriate.

Impact of the 1978 and 1986 Amendments to ADEA
The passage of the 1978 amendments to ADEA raised the mandatory retirement age from 65 to 70 and created another environmental factor impinging upon the ability of

higher education to manage its faculty resources. Those amendments had the potential impact of adding five years to the careers of many tenured faculty, although they exempted higher education from the guidelines for retirement at age 70 for tenured faculty until July 1, 1982, presumably to allow colleges and universities time to prepare for the future effects of the act (Hughes 1981, p. 213).

At about the time of the passage of the 1978 amendments, a spate of studies attempted to forecast the impact of that legislation on faculty staffing for higher education (Corwin and Knepper 1978; Fernandez 1978; Patton 1979; Simpson 1979; Tillinghast, Nelson, and Warren, Inc. 1979). The purpose of the studies varied slightly, but the questions that were addressed generally involved two major issues: institutions' ability to maintain vitality at a time of retrenchment or stability and the problems of prospective faculty members attempting to enter academic employment during the next decade (Corwin and Knepper 1978, p. 4).

Several studies predicated their assessment of the potential impact of the 1978 changes on the relatively young age of the professoriate at the time of passage of the amendments. In one study, for example, the median age of the faculties was 42, with 73 percent of the faculty under 50 years of age and only 8 percent over age 60 (Corwin and Knepper 1978, p. 14). Another stated that with a median age of 42 for faculty in the late 1970s, the median age for the professoriate would not reach 50 to 52 until about 1995 (Novotny 1981, p. 2). The implication of this observation is that the natural turnover in faculty positions because of retirements would be relatively minimal until near the year 2000.

With the passage of H.R. 4154 in October 1986, the Age Discrimination in Employment Act of 1967 was amended to remove any age as a mandatory retirement age, effective January 1, 1987. Provisions in the legislation would make exceptions to this effective date for certain employees covered under collective bargaining agreements and a seven-year exemption for faculty members serving under a contract of unlimited tenure (to expire December 31, 1993). The seven-year exemption for tenured faculty provides institutions with the opportunity to continue current practices of invoking mandatory retirement at age 70 for tenured faculty for that period of time or to immediately uncap the retirement age, as will be required on January 1, 1994 (P. L. 99–592).

In response to the 1978 amendments, about 85 percent of the institutions participating in TIAA/CREF (Teachers Insurance and Annuity Association/College Retirement Equity Fund) plans ignored the four-year exemption and began using 70 as their mandatory retirement age (Calvin 1984, p. 4). In addition, participating faculty are retiring earlier than they were 10 years ago. In 1985, 35 percent of TIAA/CREF participants started to collect their annuity incomes between the ages of 56 and 63, compared to 24 percent of participants in that age range in 1975. Conversely, 55 percent started annuity income at 65 or older in 1985, compared to 71 percent in 1976 (NACUBO 1986b). In view of these figures, the effect that the uncapping legislation will have on retirement patterns is problematic for higher education.

Tenure Status of Faculty
The tenure status of faculty is another important variable to be considered when addressing the issue of flexibility and/or financial constraints on institutions. According to a recent study of the problems of flexibility on college campuses, 94 percent of American four-year colleges and universities have a tenure system, and 57 percent of all full-time faculty at those institutions are tenured (Mortimer, Bagshaw, and Masland 1985, p. 12). The tenure ratio on campus is an important variable to an institution in an environment in which steady-state or declining enrollment dictates that no increase in the number of faculty can take place and that, in fact, some reduction may be required for financial reasons.

An additional problem created by high tenure ratios is that institutions are reticent to award tenure to qualified junior faculty, thus creating an environment in which those faculty members are cycled in and out of institutions as academic nomads (Chronister 1984, p. 7). A consequence of this lack of opportunity for employment stability in academe is the possibility that very talented individuals are not considering the professoriate as a viable career. Although regional and institutional differences exist, it has been anticipated that net additions to the professoriate will be minimal for much of the remainder of this century (Carnegie Council 1980, p. 305). Reflecting the concern of many institutions that tenuring reduces staffing flexibility is a recent report indicating that during the 1984–85 year, colleges and universities were as likely to hire new faculty in term or contract positions as they were to hire them in tenure-track positions (El-Khawas 1986, p. 5).

Projections on potential faculty turnover for the period 1985 to 2009, using a variety of assumptions, foresee a need to replace approximately two-thirds of the faculty of 1985 during the 25-year period (Bowen and Schuster 1986, p. 198). Institutions are encouraged to move with caution and tact in assessing the need for faculty turnover and in instituting programs to meet short-term and long-range staffing needs.

Financial Implications of the Age and Tenure Status of Faculty

The financial implications of the current age and tenure status of faculty, in terms of costs of compensation, have been exacerbated by the amendments to ADEA, because of the potential years of added employment for higher-paid senior faculty (Corwin and Knepper 1978, p. 25). In addition to the growth in the salary level of faculty, a continuing increase in the costs of fringe benefits has become a significant factor. For faculty at the professor level, average academic-year salaries rose from $18,314 in 1970–71 to $35,470 in 1982–83, an increase of 93.7 percent. During the same time, the average costs of fringe benefits associated with those salaries grew from 10.2 percent of salary to 16.2 percent (American Council on Education 1984, p. 124). Much of the increase in costs of benefits is attributable to health benefits and social security taxes.

As a share of the total institutional budget for current operations, it is not uncommon for personnel costs, including faculty compensation, to amount to 60 to 70 percent of an institution's expenditures. Many institutions find that by replacing senior-level faculty members with entry-level faculty members, they can partially control total costs for faculty compensation.

Students' Changing Curricular Interests

The ability of institutions to respond to evolving societal needs and students' changing curricular interests and needs has serious implications for institutions during periods of constrained faculty resources. Although the impact of these conditions varies among institutions, the influence of students' changing preferences is a factor with which colleges and universities must deal. Between 1969 and 1984, the percentage distribution of undergraduate enrollments by major had registered some dramatic changes across fields and within fields (Carnegie Foundation 1985). Based on data for 1969, 1976, and 1984, student enrollments in occupational-professional programs had fluctuated from 38 to 58 to 50 percent of total enrollments, respectively. For the humanities, the percentage of enrollments had declined from 18 percent to 5 percent over the 15 years, while enrollments in the physical sciences and mathematics fluctuated from 17 to 8 to 22 percent, respectively (p. 31). The most dramatic shifts in choice of major have occurred at the less selective liberal arts colleges (p. 32). Many institutions are finding that highly specialized, tenured faculty who were hired during the years of major growth in enrollment are less resilient in accommodating evolving and changing program needs dictated by fluctuations in students' career interests.

Faculty Morale
It is generally accepted that the quality and vitality of colleges and universities are directly related to the quality and vitality of their faculty. In recent years, a number of studies have documented a malaise within the professoriate that threatens the quality and vitality of colleges and universities and their ability to respond to the challenges of the next several decades (Jacobson 1985; Schuster and Bowen 1985). Nearly 40 percent of faculty are less enthusiastic about their careers than they were earlier, almost 25 percent would consider a change of career, more than half would consider taking another academic position, and close to 30 percent feel trapped in their jobs (Jacobson 1985, p. 1). Contributing to this malaise among junior faculty members has been the pressure created by the recognition that even if they meet adequate academic criteria of productivity for promotion and tenure, environmental factors such as uncertain enrollments and financial constraints might mitigate against them in the award of tenure.

TABLE 1

YEARS IN WHICH INCENTIVE EARLY RETIREMENT PROGRAMS WERE ESTABLISHED, BY TYPE OF PROGRAM AND NUMBER OF INSTITUTIONS

Years	Early	Partial	Phased
Before 1975	3	3	1
1975 and 1976	1	6	2
1977 and 1978	1	1	5
1979 and 1980	4	3	3
1981 and 1982	12	5	3
1983 and 1984	6	2	2
Total	**27**	**20**	**16**

Source: Chronister and Trainer 1985a, p. 28.

Institutional Interest in Incentive Early Retirement Programs

In view of these problems and issues, a large number of colleges and universities have been seeking programs that will create turnover in faculty positions toward the goal of reducing staff, reducing the institution's tenure ratio, providing for the reallocation of positions, and/or providing for renewal of the faculty through recruitment of new faculty. The implementation of incentive early retirement programs for faculty is one strategy that a growing number of institutions have been using to achieve these goals (Chronister and Trainer 1985a; Kepple 1984). Data gathered in a study of 51 public universities provide information on the growth of incentive early retirement programs in recent years. It is evident from table 1 that activity in program development and implementation heightened at about the time of the enactment of amendments to ADEA in 1978.

A study of incentive early retirement programs in 252 liberal arts colleges found that 15.5 percent (39) of the colleges had an established program; furthermore, an additional 20.2 percent (51) of the colleges' presidents indicated that they expected to have programs established by June 1985 (Kepple 1984, p. 61). Viewed from a different perspective, only one of the institutions had an incentive early retirement program in 1971, but 11 colleges had established such programs during the first six months of 1983 (p. 63).

It is difficult to determine the number of institutions of higher education offering incentive early retirement options to faculty, but estimates range from about 100 institutions (Palmer 1984, p. 23) to 25 to 30 percent of all colleges and universities (Watkins 1985, p. 21). With the abolition of mandatory retirement, however, it can be expected that many colleges and universities will express a renewed interest in incentive early retirement programs as essential management strategies.

INCENTIVE EARLY RETIREMENT PROGRAMS:
Concepts and Definitions

Early retirement has received a significant amount of attention in higher education in recent years, although the concept itself is not new in academic circles. Faculty retirement before an institution's designated regular or mandatory age has been part of the higher education scene for many years. It is during the past decade that the development of incentive early retirement programs, as a personnel management strategy, has gained the increased interest of institutional leaders. The influence of the multitude of factors cited in the preceding section has led an increasing number of institutions to seek a means of inducing a number of faculty to retire early. These strategies, designed to facilitate the earlier separation from full-time employment, are generally referred to as "incentive early retirement programs."

Incentive early retirement programs must be structured so that the decision to retire at an early age is at the discretion of the individual. Therefore, incentive early retirement programs can be described as any arrangement between an employer and an employee designed to provide tangible inducements in the form of a monetary or an in-kind reward for early retirement (Jenny 1974, p. 8). Such programs are designed to be voluntary and the incentives, or tangible inducements, therefore structured so that faculty members identify themselves as candidates for participation (Patton 1983c, p. 1a). Early retirement programs must, by virtue of the Age Discrimination in Employment Act, be voluntary in nature (P. L. 99–592, Age Discrimination in Employment Act Amendments of 1986).

Incentive early retirement programs must be structured so that the decision to retire at an early age is at the discretion of the individual.

Program Structures
Early retirement programs generally fall into one of two classifications—ad hoc plans or formal plans (Kepple 1984, p. 5). Although an institution might establish general guidelines for an ad hoc program, a set level of incentives is not prescribed. Under an ad hoc approach, each early retirement is negotiated separately with the individual faculty member. The advantage to institutions of an ad hoc program is the flexibility to use limited resources targeted at areas of greatest need. The faculty member has the opportunity to bargain for benefits that might not normally be part of formal early retirement programs. The disadvantages of the ad hoc approach are that it does not provide a

very effective base for long-range institutional planning, and it has the potential for raising issues of equity among faculty who express an interest in retiring early but are unable to obtain an incentive to participate.

Formal incentive early retirement programs are plans with specific guidelines, policies, and procedures under which any faculty member meeting the established criteria for eligibility may apply to participate. The advantages of formal programs are that all potential faculty participants within specified classes are treated under the same guidelines, and the institution has a better opportunity to effectively project costs per faculty member for the program. A perceived disadvantage of formal programs is that once established, they do not provide for negotiation of benefits to meet individual faculty interests beyond what is provided in the plan, which might be a disadvantage for the institution if a faculty member in a field in which a reduction is desired or a faculty member desiring to leave academe would choose to retire early but with incentive benefits different from those provided in the formal program. At the other extreme, the standard benefits provided by the institution might unwittingly attract into early retirement faculty whom the institution would choose not to lose.

Incentive Plan Options
Whether a plan is ad hoc or formal, it will most likely include one or more of the following incentives individually or in combination. In fact, most incentive early retirement programs on college and university campuses combine the following options in some way because of the need to meet a variety of economic and professional concerns and institutional objectives (Chronister and Trainer 1985a). For each strategy, careful attention must be paid to how the incentives are structured to comply with requirements dictated by the Tax Reform Act of 1986.

Severance pay or lump-sum payment
Under these options, an individual receives a financial bonus for voluntarily retiring early. The basis for the payment is normally some percentage of base pay. For example, under a lump-sum plan, an individual might receive 150 percent of his or her current salary for retiring at a specified age, say 62. Options under this type of incentive

include a lump-sum payment, a tax-sheltered payment, or deferred payments over a number of years (Patton 1979, pp. 11–12).

For the faculty member without concerns about inflation or with an immediate need for cash, this option might be most desirable. For the institution, the program is relatively simple to administer and can be relatively low cost (Kepple 1984, p. 6). This option, however, if not carefully structured, has the potential to create a significant tax burden for faculty members (Price Waterhouse 1986, pp. 83–90).

Liberalization of the actuarial reduction
This incentive is a common one: An individual who retires early receives the full, or nearly full, value of his or her pension annuity as if employment had been continued until the normal retirement age. For the employer to provide the employee an unreduced benefit formula at age 60 in contrast to what it would have been had the employee worked until age 65 would necessitate an increase of approximately 50 percent in the employer's cost (Patton 1983c, p. 3a).

Annuity enhancements
Annuity enhancement can take several forms, but in each case the enhancement is intended to boost the retirement income to approximately the level that would have been achieved had the faculty member remained employed until the regular or target retirement age. It is accomplished by providing an additional annuity that supplements the individual's original retirement annuity or by providing an interim payment that permits delay of the start of payout of the original retirement annuity until a future date.

Two approaches to annuity enhancement have been used in early retirement programs: "annuity premium continuation" or "supplemental annuity purchase." Annuity premium continuation is an arrangement that continues payments to an employee's annuity contract during a period of phased retirement or continuation of salary. It is also sometimes offered to terminating employees who are receiving payments in lieu of salary (Heller 1979, p. 5).

The supplemental annuity purchase is normally used to increase the accumulation under an annuity contract at a specific age. For example, a person retiring at age 62 might receive a supplemental annuity that would bring the level of accumulation up to what would have been achieved at age 65 if the employee had not retired early. A supplemental annuity purchase is normally accomplished by a lump-sum contribution at the point of early retirement or by a series of annual contributions before the employee's early retirement. This annual contribution method is less likely to create tax problems for the faculty member (Heller 1979, p. 6).

Bridging benefit programs

A variation of the annuity enhancement plan is to have the faculty member retire at the early retirement target age, begin to draw social security, and begin to receive a supplement from the institution to bring net income up to a predetermined objective. The institution might or might not continue to pay into the early retiree's pension fund during the early retirement years (Chronister and Trainer 1985b; White 1981).

Cash supplements paid to early retirees during a specified number of years before regular retirement are commonly referred to as "bridging payments" (Chronister and Trainer 1985b; White 1981, pp. 8–12). The advantage of this plan for the early retiree is that he or she does not draw down the annuity corpus until a later age, say 65 or 70, thus ensuring a significantly larger yearly annuity payment until death. The disadvantage of the program is its normally high expense to the institution relative to other types of early retirement incentives (Kepple 1984, p. 8). Institutions that have defined benefit programs and/or that do not participate in social security should not attempt bridging programs; such institutions should consider annuity supplement plans (Patton 1983c, p. 4a).

Phased and partial retirement plans

In phased or partial retirement programs, faculty members voluntarily retire in exchange for part-time employment that might be provided with other financial incentives. Generally, through some combination of part-time salary, social security income, reduced income tax liability, and/or annuity payments, the early retiree can obtain a disposable income equal to or greater than his former salary for full-time employment (Kepple 1984, p. 6).

Advantages to the retiree of such programs include a gradual disengagement from full-time employment with the possibility of retaining other benefits, such as office space and support services (Walker 1972). Advantages to the institution are the release of a full-time position and the related compensation costs.

A distinction that can be drawn between the two types of programs is that in phased retirement, retirees do not draw against their retirement annuity funds and the institution may continue to contribute to that fund during the period of phased employment. In a partial retirement program, retirees draw benefits but are permitted to maintain a limited part-time employment status as part of the incentive (Chronister and Trainer 1985a, p. 28).

Other perquisites

Included among such benefits might be continued use of an office, photocopying services, and secretarial support and continued participation in group health and life insurance programs. These incentives are usually most effective when used in conjunction with other options (Patton 1979, p. 13).

Key Concepts, Terms, and Definitions

A number of key concepts and terms must be recognized and understood by those who are involved in the development and administration of incentive early retirement programs.

A fundamental consideration facing faculty members who are candidates for incentive early retirement programs is the "compensation" package that has been their source of support during the employment years. Compensation includes both salary and fringe benefits. Although salary, which is evident in the pay check, is most often recognized as a prime consideration for the individual debating the decision to retire early, fringe benefits cannot be overlooked.

Fringe benefits can be classified into one of three basic groups—statutory benefits, voluntary benefits, and support benefits (Kepple 1984, pp. 22–23). Statutory benefits are benefits required by law and generally include social security and workman's compensation. Voluntary benefits are those that the institution chooses to offer or that may be required by contract. Examples of such benefits include professional travel, medical insurance, disability insurance, and contributions to a retirement fund. Support benefits might include office space, secretarial support, access to scientific equipment, parking, computer and library services, and access to athletic and cultural events.

A fundamental economic issue for faculty considering early retirement is the "foregone compensation," or amount of income and fringe benefits lost by retiring early.

Although compensation is viewed as a current reward received in exchange for work, "deferred compensation" is a strategy that provides for payments after cessation of full-time employment (Heller 1979, p. 3). This type of plan normally provides a maximum amount of nontaxable income.

Another strategy that deals with the impact of loss of income is referred to as "salary continuation"; it involves payment of all or part of an employee's salary for a period of time after termination of employment (Heller 1979, p. 6). Salary continuation is one of the incentives that might be a component of a formal "bridging" early retirement program; it can also be a negotiable item for an institution that uses the individually negotiated ad hoc contract approach to facilitating early retirement.

The literature on early retirement refers to the terms "normal" retirement age and "mandatory" retirement age. "Normal" retirement age is used in retirement planning to designate an age for setting retirement income objectives and contribution rates. The designated normal age might be earlier than or might coincide with the "mandatory" retirement age of 70, which is the age at which it has been permissible to require an employee to retire under the 1978 amendments to ADEA. Under the 1986 amendments to ADEA, institutions of higher education can continue to retire tenured faculty at age 70 until January 1, 1994, although untenured faculty and other employees were covered by the uncapping requirements as of January 1, 1987. Therefore, until January 1, 1994, institutions that take advantage of the exemption for tenured faculty will have a mandatory retirement age for some of their employees and no such designation for others. After the seven-year exemption expires, a mandatory retirement age will no longer be part of the lexicon for describing retirement planning. Plans in which the normal retirement age is set within the ages of 65 to 70 appear to conform with reasonable practice.

When an incentive early retirement program is in the developmental stage, an institution must determine whether the offering will be "continuous" or made for only a specified time period. Limited-period early retirement program options are commonly referred to as "open window" or "window" offerings. For example, a window program might state that the incentive program will be made available from July 1, 1986, until June 30, 1987, to faculty who meet the eligibility requirements of a specified minimum age, such as 62, and a minimum number of years of service, such as 25. Once the period is over, no more early retirement incentives will be available. A variation of the window program is to open the enrollment to a specified age group that, if affected employees do not enroll during that age "window," will lose the opportunity to participate at a later age (Chronister and Trainer 1985b). Window programs provide the institution with a control of programs that a continuous program offering does not have unless the nondelimited program is canceled or revoked. A window offering also tends to reinforce the notion that an early retirement program is designed as a benefit to the institution rather than an ongoing faculty benefit program.

Retirement Annuity Plans
A characteristic of nearly all incentive early retirement programs is that they are integrated to one degree or another with an institution's existing retirement benefit programs. Retirement benefit programs have two fundamental classifications: "defined contribution plans" and "defined benefit plans." An understanding of the differences between these classifications is basic to incentive program planning.

Defined contribution plans are those plans in which the amount of the retirement annuity a retiree receives is based upon the level of employee/employer contributions made to the employee's retirement fund (account) plus the investment earnings on those contributions. The ultimate benefit derived by the retiree depends on the investment performance of the accumulated assets and therefore places the individual in the position of assuming the investment risk (Commission on College Retirement 1986, p. 12). Length of service is not the major determinant of size of the pension, but the age at which an individual chooses to begin retirement will affect the annual annuity payment because of actuarial considerations (Jenny 1981). The TIAA/CREF plan is an example of a defined contribution program. Institutions with defined contribution retirement programs that are attempting to meet concerns about post-retirement income of faculty contemplating early retirement will be best served by providing an annuity enhancement.

In defined benefit plans, benefits are derived based upon a formula that uses age at retirement, number of years of participation in the plan, and a salary figure that might be the average of several years of highest salary or the last year(s) of service. The annual pension is then a percentage of this average salary (Jenny 1981). Public employee pension plans are usually defined benefit programs. Two attractive features of these plans are the predictability of the benefit as one nears normal retirement age and the possibility of building early retirement incentives into the structure of the offerings (Commission on College Retirement 1986, p. 12).

Colleges and universities should be sure that their plans provide for early retirement at age 55 or later. Without this provision, early retirees who wish to begin receiving retirement payments will face a penalty for premature distribution (Ernst & Whinney 1986, p. 129).

Incentive early retirement programs at institutions with defined benefit retirement plans should be designed to overcome some or all of the retirement service credit employees lose by retiring early. The impact of the loss of the retirement service credit in formulas used to calculate retirement annuity benefits is easily documented (Reinhard 1981). A study of the early retirement incentive program of California state universities and colleges found that by participating in the offering, which provided two years of additional unearned service credit toward their retirement annuities, faculty increased their annual retirement annuity by 2.18 to 4.84 percent of the average salary paid the employee during the three years immediately preceding early retirement (Reinhard 1981, p. 12).

Health Insurance

Among the major concerns for faculty considering early retirement are the questions that surround personal health and postretirement health insurance coverage (Chronister and Trainer 1985b, p. 197; Felicetti 1982, p. 24). This concern is well grounded: People age 65 and over are more likely to be hospitalized, have longer hospital stays, and make more visits to doctors than younger people. Per capita spending on personal health care for persons aged 65 and over was $4,200 in 1984, nearly four times the amount spent for individuals under 65 (TIAA 1986, p. 3).

During preretirement years, health insurance for faculty members, whether the cost is paid for by the institution or shared by the faculty member and the institution, provides a known, regular payment for an unknown and potentially large expense in the event of serious illness. For early retirees, the concern with health insurance involves two factors: the potential loss of the institution's subsidy of such insurance and the potential loss of the group rate to the individual if the retiree must provide the coverage personally (Chronister and Trainer 1985b, p. 197).

The age at which faculty members begin early retirement in an institution's incentive program has implications for the degree to which health insurance is a key factor. For most retired persons aged 65 and over, Medicare provides needed continuing health insurance. All persons aged 65 and older who are eligible for social security retirement benefits are automatically eligible for Part A coverage, which is hospital insurance without additional cost. Since 1972, individuals in the same age bracket who are not eligible for social security benefits may enroll in Medicare Part A if they also enroll in Part B (supplementary medical insurance) and pay a monthly premium (King and Cook 1980, p. 192).

Medicare assists individuals to meet some medical costs, but it by no means covers all such expenses. In recent years, Medicare coverage has paid for slightly less than half of total personal health care spending for people age 65 and over (TIAA 1986, p. 3). It is evident that faculty members age 65 or older considering participation in an early retirement program will seek health insurance coverage to supplement the benefits of Medicare. In many instances, it is expected that such coverage will be at institutional

Colleges and universities should be sure that their plans provide for early retirement at age 55 or later.

expense as part of the incentive program (Chronister and Trainer 1985b, p. 197). One bridging program, for example, provided continued group health insurance for participants at institutional expense at the same rate as for active employees (White 1981, p. 9).

The provision of early retirement programs with a threshold age for eligibility earlier than age 65 requires the institution to make a decision: to provide group health insurance coverage as part of the incentive program for a specified number of years at institutional expense, to provide the option for early retirees at their own expense to continue in the group plan, or to require that individual retirees provide continued health insurance coverage for themselves. A study of approximately 20 early and phased retirement programs by the National Association of College and University Business Officers (NACUBO) indicated that most institutions' plans cover the early retiree's full health insurance cost, including that of the spouse and eligible dependents until the age of normal retirement or death, whichever occurs first (Covert-McGrath 1984a, p. 13). It should also be noted that institutions can provide health insurance to retired faculty at a relatively modest cost when an individual is included under the institution's group health care plan and Medicare.

Life Insurance
Life insurance is another benefit that some institutions include in their incentive programs. The NACUBO study also found that the options for institutional payment of life insurance ranged from no provision of the benefit for early retirees to the provision of coverage payments until the retiree reaches normal retirement age or mandatory retirement age, including providing the retiree with the opportunity to enter the institution's plan at his or her own expense (Covert-McGrath 1984a, p. 15).

Relevant Federal Statutes and Regulations
Several federal statutes and regulatory standards directly affect the incentives and criteria that can be used in early retirement programs. Although incentive early retirement programs have been in existence at many institutions for a number of years, federal legislation enacted during 1986

has changed a number of the rules under which such programs must function. The following citations underscore the need for adequate legal and tax counsel in the development and implementation of such programs. State statutes must also be recognized as they may apply to incentive early retirement programs.

ADEA, which made it unlawful for an employer to discriminate against an employee because of age, was amended in 1986 to abolish mandatory retirement because of age, effective January 1, 1987 (P. L. 99–592). A section of the act provides an exception, repealed effective December 31, 1993, to this uncapping for a period of seven years for faculty members serving under a contract of unlimited tenure. Certain exceptions were also provided for employees covered under collective bargaining agreements. The ADEA exemption that has permitted the mandatory retirement age for bona fide executives and high-ranking policy-making employees was retained.

Institutions with tenure systems face a major issue in deciding whether to invoke the seven-year exemption for tenured faculty. Invoking the exemption has the potential of creating two classes of employees until January 1, 1994: those tenured faculty in the exempt class who can be forced to retire at age 70, and those not covered by the exemption who can continue to work past age 70.

Institutions with existing incentive early retirement programs are also required to review their programs to ensure that such programs comply with the amended ADEA, as well as the following statutes.

The Employee Retirement Income Security Act of 1974 (ERISA), which was enacted to protect the pension rights of employees, is another major piece of federal legislation directly affecting early retirement programs (Patton 1979, p. 163). Early retirement programs will be influenced by how they fit within the ERISA requirements in terms of "eligibility and participation, vesting, funding, and reporting and disclosure. . ." (Heller 1979, p. 1).

ERISA has four titles; Titles I and II contain the provisions relevant to early retirement annuity supplements. Title I deals with employee benefit plans, while Title II contains the rules governing employee retirement plans that meet the tax qualification requirements of the Internal Revenue Code (Shapiro 1980, p. 175). The viable alterna-

tives under ERISA for providing early retirement annuity supplements are tax-sheltered annuities, unfunded deferred compensation, or a combination of the two (p. 178). It is important that institutions consult the regulations in ERISA as a program for early retirement options is developed.

Of significance to the use of supplemental annuity plans in early retirement programs at tax-exempt institutions are the provisions of Section 403(b) of the Internal Revenue Code. This section provides for the exclusion from an employee's gross income of amounts paid by employers toward the purchase of an annuity. The annual contributions that may be excluded from the employee's gross income must not exceed the exclusion allowance as set forth in Section 415 of the Code (Patton 1979, p. 166).

Among the changes specified in the Tax Reform Act of 1986 were several that are directly applicable to incentive early retirement programs (P. L. 99–514, October 22, 1986). An employee's annual elective contribution under a tax-sheltered annuity program is limited to the greater of $9,500 or the cap on 401(k) salary reductions (currently $7,000) as indexed for inflation (Ernst & Whinney 1986, p. 117). In addition, tax-sheltered annuity plans known as 403(b)s will be subject to the nondiscrimination requirements of other qualified plans beginning January 1, 1989 (NACUBO 1986c, p. 20).

Limitations on eligible deferred compensation plans will generally allow for deferral of the lesser of $7,500 or 33⅓ percent of compensation. This amount will be reduced by the amount of elective deferrals to tax-sheltered annuities (Peat, Marwick 1986, p. 48).

Legislation included as part of the Omnibus Budget Reconciliation Act of 1986 has a provision dealing with pension benefits for employees who continue to work past the normal retirement age (P. L. 99–509). The legislation prohibits employers from discontinuing or reducing benefit accruals or contributions to retirement plans for employees who attain the "normal" retirement age under the plan. The legislation takes effect for plan years beginning on or after January 1, 1988, and applies to both defined benefit and defined contribution plans. For plans affected by collective bargaining agreements, the law is effective on the date that

the last agreement terminates or January 1, 1990, whichever comes first (NACUBO 1986a, p. 9).

In addition, it is important for institutions and individual
faculty members to recognize the potential financial liabili-
ties of federal income tax regulations if early retirement
financial incentives are not appropriately structured and
administered. It is also important for institutions and faculty members to be cognizant of current social security law
as it may affect retirement benefits.

ASSESSING THE FEASIBILITY OF ESTABLISHING AN EARLY RETIREMENT PROGRAM

Assessing the feasibility of establishing an early retirement program—whether on an individual college or university campus or in a system of campuses—is a multidimensional undertaking. The development of an incentive early retirement plan must be justified on the basis of institutional needs and objectives and the relevant characteristics of the faculty and staff to whom it is addressed. Formal early retirement programs vary widely in character and purpose among the many institutions that offer them, but they are "a function of the culture of our institutions" (Watkins 1985, p. 19). The development of an incentive early retirement program must take into consideration the "culture" of the institution for which it is being developed and whether the institution is public or private.

One question is frequently asked about planning for incentive early retirement programs: "Who should be involved in assessing the need for and developing the program?" The answer is generically simple but institutionally complex. In a generic sense, several constituencies must be involved in assessment: the governing board, which ultimately must approve it; the chief executive officer and his or her academic and financial advisors, who will likely propose the program to the governing board; and the faculty, whose interest and support must be cultivated if the program is to succeed.

The Role of Faculty

The question of who should be involved and to what extent most frequently centers on the role of the faculty in the development of the program. Each institution must resolve the questions based on its own structure of governance and political reality and on the objectives for the program. One rule of thumb appears valid: The broader the target of the program, the more faculty input desired. The rule can be illustrated by two examples. According to the president of a college whose interest in an early retirement program was only to remove a few poorly performing faculty members:

I did not get involved in the process early enough. A faculty committee appointed by me to review the options ended up proposing a very generous fringe benefit–type incentive when all we really needed was to attract two or three specific faculty into retirement. It became a difficult political problem to fully reject the committee's recommendation (Kepple 1984, p. 163).

In this case, active faculty participation provided a larger incentive than needed and might have been counterproductive to encouraging the "right" faculty to retire. In other cases, faculty participation has been more successful.

One institution used a committee comprised of faculty members and administrators representing various formal committees of the institution's faculty senate (budget policy, tenure and academic freedom, health and welfare, and administrative policies) (Clevenger and Chronister 1986, p. 10). In this case, the initiative for the study of the feasibility of establishing an early retirement program came from the faculty senate at a time when enrollment was not a problem but demographic projections for several years into the future forecast a probable decline.

The use of ad hoc faculty committees, appointed by the institutional administration and operating outside the formal faculty governance structure, is another strategy (Chronister and Trainer 1985b, p. 191). In one case, such a committee was appointed by the academic vice president in response to concerns expressed by academic deans about future staffing flexibility in the face of steady-state enrollment and faculty staffing. The committee was charged to report back to the academic vice president and the deans on how well they perceived an incentive early retirement program would meet the concerns of the deans and what such a program should include if they felt a program would be beneficial.

In contrast, the development of an incentive early retirement program at a West Coast institution was an effort of the institution's administration, with the faculty senate subcommittee on retirement serving in an advisory capacity (Clevenger and Chronister 1986, pp. 19–20). A midwestern university experienced the situation of having an incentive early retirement program that had been designed by the administration but was receiving little interest or support from faculty. Many faculty felt that the program was extremely costly, both in actual dollars and in the potential loss of large numbers of faculty. In response to this lack of faculty support for the existing program, an ad hoc faculty committee was appointed to restudy the situation and to develop a new program that would more adequately meet institutional needs and respond to faculty concerns (Clevenger and Chronister 1986, p. 26). The result of the ad hoc committee's study was the design and implementation of an incentive program that is viewed as an institutional benefit program rather than a faculty benefit offering.

At Rhodes College, the planned objective of an incentive program was to obtain the early retirements of 15 percent of the faculty to provide enhanced academic flexibility (American Council on Education 1986). The approach was to encourage faculty involvement in the development of the program. A committee appointed by the president, chaired by a respected member of the faculty, and comprised of faculty, administrators, and representatives of the board of trustees was able to survey the faculty to determine what specific incentives would attract enough faculty into early retirement. The process publicized the plan, thus encouraging many faculty to begin thinking about the possibility of early retirement. The committee also proposed retirement counseling sessions, which ultimately proved to be an important element in individual faculty decisions. The result of this faculty involvement was an incentive package that enabled the college to exceed its goal of early retirement of 15 percent of the faculty.

The committee also proposed retirement counseling sessions, which ultimately proved to be an important element in individual faculty decisions.

Objectives of an Incentive Program

The key question in determining who should be involved and to what extent in the development of an early retirement program is what objective or objectives of the institution might be assisted by establishing an incentive early retirement program. Objectives can be classified within three broad areas: academic, fiscal, and fringe benefits. Most often, an institution has multiple, interrelated objectives it wants to accomplish (Chronister and Trainer 1985b; Clevenger and Chronister 1986; Kepple 1984, p. 162).

The following examples are actual objectives used by various colleges and universities:

- **Academic objectives**
  - Maintain average age of faculty, or lower average age from _____ to _____.

- Reallocate positions from overstaffed to under-staffed departments.
- Increase overall quality of the faculty in a buyer's market.
- Provide more opportunity for young faculty to obtain tenure.
- Retain the services of a prestigious faculty member, who might otherwise retire fully, through a phased retirement plan.
- Add new blood to a specific program or programs or to the entire faculty.
- Increase the representation of minorities or women on the faculty.
- **Fiscal objectives**
  - Reduce the college's expense budget.
  - Reallocate salary savings to nonacademic purposes, such as financial aid.
  - Reduce or hold constant the student/faculty ratio.
- **Fringe benefit objectives**
  - Provide financial security for senior faculty members at retirement.
  - Provide benefits to allow a faculty member to retire at age 65 (or 55, 62, 67, or whenever).
  - Permit faculty to reduce teaching loads gradually, rather than having their appointments terminate abruptly through a full retirement (Kepple 1984, p. 162).

Once objectives are established, the next question that needs to be answered is whether an incentive early retirement program is an appropriate tool to use to meet the institution's objectives. That question raises several others.

Is the faculty likely to retire at a pace that will assist the institution in meeting its objectives without the expense of an incentive? Simply graphing faculty ages may answer this question, as illustrated in figure 1.

If the objective of both institutions depicted in figure 1 is to reduce the percentage of tenured faculty, Institution A might be able to accomplish its goal without providing any incentives for early retirement because of the proportion of the faculty who are age 65 and over. Institution B, however, might not be able to reduce the tenure ratio without a very expensive incentive program aimed at a relatively

FIGURE 1
SAMPLE GRAPH OF FACULTY AGES

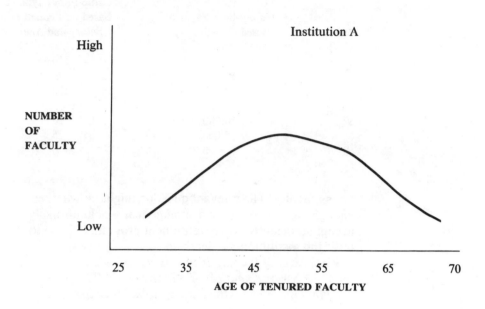

Institution A

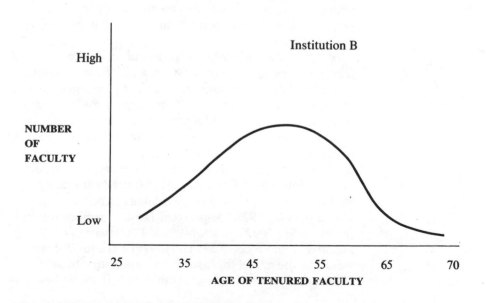

Institution B

FIGURE 2
EXAMPLES OF TWO FORMAL PLANS

Age	Plan A (Lump-Sum Payment Based on Age Only)	Plan B (Lump-Sum Payment Based on Percent of Salary and Age)
45–62	$60,000	150%
63–64	50,000	125
65	40,000	100
66	30,000	75
67	10,000	50
68	5,000	25
69–70	0	0

young faculty. The relevant question might be whether enough faculty are in the age range that would normally accept an incentive early retirement program (55–67) to meet the institution's objectives.

What level of funding is the institution willing to commit to an early retirement program, and could this funding be used in a more cost-efficient way to achieve the same objectives?

Assuming an incentive early retirement program appears viable, *what form should the incentive early retirement program take?* The answer to that question depends on several others:

Is the institution's target highly paid faculty or low-paid faculty? Depending on the answer, an incentive formula could be devised to encourage the "right" group of faculty to retire early. For example, if the target is low-paid faculty, the incentive should not be structured based on a percentage of salary. If an institution is interested in attracting lower-paid faculty into retirement, for example, it would choose a plan modeled after plan A (see figure 2). Under plan A, both a $25,000- and a $50,000-per-year faculty member would receive a $60,000 bonus to retire at age 62. Under plan B, a $25,000-per-year faculty member would receive a $37,500 bonus, while a $50,000-per-year faculty member would receive $75,000 to retire at age 62. Plan B would be the model for institutions attempting to attract higher-paid faculty into early retirement. It would be possible to take this strategy even further, tying low pay to high incentive. For example, a person making $25,000 at age 62 would receive a $50,000 incentive, while a person making $50,000 would receive a $25,000 incentive.

Another approach to the issue is reflected in Stanford University's program. On the assumption that salary level is an indication of quality, Stanford University's plan is aimed at faculty age 55 and above who are making *less* than the median departmental salary (Taylor and Coolidge 1974, p. 185).

The strategy of targeting "low-paid" faculty might have objectionable side effects. For an institution that intends to cover the cost of the incentive and/or hire replacement faculty from the salary funds freed by early retirements, significantly less money will be available from the retirements of lower-paid than higher-paid faculty (Weiler 1981, p. 137).

Will the institution's objectives be met if a limited number of specific faculty retire early, or is a large number of nonspecific faculty the target? If the target is a limited number of specific faculty, an ad hoc plan (a plan offered to specific faculty only and not available generally) might be the most advantageous. By using an ad hoc plan, whose incentives might include money, secretarial assistance, football tickets, part-time employment, special sabbatical leave, continued health benefits, contribution to a retirement annuity, and/or office space, the administration can negotiate with a specific individual to tailor the exact incentive necessary to obtain an early retirement.

In other cases, the target might be a large nonselect group of older faculty. For example, one college, whose goal was to increase the quality of the faculty during a buyer's market, wanted a large number of retirements within three to five years to take advantage of what it perceived as a limited opportunity (Kepple 1984, p. 135). That college chose a "formal" incentive early retirement program to accomplish its objectives.

Is the target a small number of nonspecific faculty? If so, a minimum incentive plan might encourage enough faculty to retire to meet the institution's goals. For example, one college offered a continuation of retirement annuity payments, or about 10 percent of salary per year, for several years (Kepple 1984, p. 106). Several faculty accepted the incentive early retirement program, and the institution was thus able to reach its limited goal at a very low cost.

Are the targeted faculty members in specific departments? If so, a program can be designed to allocate early retirements based on departmental priority. For example, a college might offer a limited number of early retirement slots each year, with the selection criteria for recipients of early retirement based on which departments benefit most (Clevenger and Chronister 1986, p. 27).

Is the institution prepared to offer part-time employment? If so, is the part-time position available to all faculty who choose it or only to those faculty in departments that the college believes can "accommodate" part-time positions? Several programs offer this option to faculty but only with the institution's approval (Kepple 1984, p. 7). A typical part-time program will establish a maximum part-time teaching load, such as 50 percent of the normal load, and will often limit earnings to the maximum allowed without reducing social security benefits ($6,960 in 1984) (p. 136).

Should the institution establish a specific period of time during which the faculty member may contract for an early retirement? A number of colleges attribute success with incentive early retirement programs to the fact that the college offered a highly publicized one-time-only opportunity for a limited time during which faculty could accept the incentive, contending that without a deadline, faculty would tend to postpone the decision (Kepple 1984, p. 164). In almost every case, institutions establish a limited time period during which the incentive early retirement program is available. Some institutions indicate that only one offer will be made; others indicate that the offer will run for a specific period and then will be reevaluated to determine whether it will continue. Typical offering periods range from five months to five years (p. 165).

If a limited time is available for faculty to decide whether to retire early, will the institution be willing to contract for future retirements? Would the program allow a contract today for a retirement four years from now? According to one college president:

> *Though our faculty had only six months to decide whether they wanted to take the option, we did allow*

*them to contract for an early retirement at any time in
the future. Several benefits accrued because of this policy. First, a number of "younger" faculty (50–55)
wanted to change careers. By contracting for the retirement incentive several years in the future, they could
prepare for the career change both educationally and
financially.*

*Second, the college gained the advantage of being
able to plan for both early retirements and mandatory
retirements through 1991. Shifts of faculty resources
between departments could be planned for over time,
rather than with each individual faculty termination.*

*Third, the college also gained the advantage of
recruiting early for a large number of definite openings.
Finally, the cost of the program was spread out over
eight years, allowing us to fund it from various sources,
including salary savings, gifts, and annual surplus* (Kepple 1984, p. 165).

Should single or multiple options be offered? In a survey
of liberal arts colleges in 1983, eight of the 39 respondents
offered two or more incentive early retirement plans (Kepple 1984, p. 152). Those colleges concluded that by offering
multiple options, more faculty would be attracted into
early retirement.

What age group is the target of the plan? The older the
target group, the more available are the benefits of retirement annuities, social security payments, and tax reductions. The lower the age group, the higher the college-
funded incentive necessary to overcome the lack of these
benefits.

*What limits should be established for participation in the
program?* Most plans establish requirements for specific
age, tenure status, and years of service for participation in
the plan. By the nature of the committee process, plans
can emerge that are overly restrictive—possibly counterproductive—to the institution's goals. One college, whose
major objective was to reallocate salary saved to other purposes, limited participation to faculty aged 65 through 69.
After seven years, only three out of a total of 112 faculty
chose to accept early retirement. Thus, to reach its objectives, this college might have to lower its threshold age of
participation to less than 65 (p. 94).

How complicated should the incentive formula be? Most agree that an incentive early retirement plan should "be easy to understand and simple to administer" (Chronister and Trainer 1985b, p. 198). Complicated formulas lead to misunderstanding and discourage rather than encourage faculty and their spouses from exploring the options available (Kepple 1984, p. 166).

The Use of Faculty Flow Models in Planning

Whatever the objectives of a proposed early retirement program might be, colleges and universities would do well to test the probable effects of such policy decisions by using a faculty flow model (Patton 1979, p. 116). Such models help in understanding the effects of personnel policy changes by showing the relationships between and among the variables that must be considered in assessing the potential impact of the changed policy (Mortimer, Bagshaw, and Masland 1985, p. 59). Decision makers can use a model to examine the effects of alternative policies and options on the faculty profile or demographic characteristics toward the goal of achieving institutional objectives for establishing an incentive early retirement program.

The faculty characteristics that are most often of concern to an institution considering an early retirement program and that must be considered for inclusion in the flow modeling include age, tenure status, and possibly salary (Chronister and Trainer 1985b, p. 195). Other characteristics that might need to be considered are years of service to the institution, quality of teaching, and teaching discipline.

In addition to these characteristics, the recent historical rate of turnover of faculty must be determined to understand the dynamics of "faculty flow" and to project the profile and characteristics of the faculty if no program intervention is undertaken. Faculty turnover, or separation from an institution of higher education, can be classified as voluntary or involuntary. Voluntary separations include retirement before the mandatory age and other individually initiated separations. Involuntary separations include death, denial of tenure, nonrenewal of term contracts, and mandatory retirement (Chronister and Trainer 1985b, p. 195).

The key questions that a college or university might ask as it assesses the feasibility of establishing an early retirement program must relate directly to the goals and objectives for which it is considering establishing the program. If the purpose is to reduce the tenure ratio on campus, the question might be, "What will our tenure ratio be in five or ten years if we do not attempt to induce senior tenured faculty to retire before the mandatory retirement age or at an age earlier than the faculty member might have planned to retire?" Another question might be concerned with the number of new hires that is possible, under stable staffing conditions, if the institution were to increase the number of retirements each year by inducing early retirements from a specified age cohort of faculty. Flow models can assist in projecting alternatives that provide possible answers to these questions.

Several types of flow models are available for use in projecting the characteristics of cohorts of faculty to some future period of time. Most such models are heuristic in that they depict a logical relationship among variables but depend upon the decision maker to guide the modeling process (Mortimer, Bagshaw, and Masland 1985, p. 61).

A common approach to modeling uses a finite number of states, and the movement of faculty from one state to another in the model is based upon a set of probabilities that are set forth in the program of the model (Chronister and Trainer 1985b, p. 195; Mortimer, Bagshaw, and Masland 1985, p. 61). These flow models (Markov models) trace the movements of faculty through a series of categories referred to as states, and the choice of the number of states in the model varies based upon the faculty characteristics and variables being studied and the question(s) being addressed. Such institutions as Stanford University, Oregon State University, and the Pennsylvania State University have used Markov models (Mortimer, Bagshaw, and Masland 1985, pp. 62–63).

A Markov-type model was used in the case study of the development of one early retirement program reported in the literature (Chronister and Trainer 1985b). The institution was attempting to assess the possible effect of an early retirement program that would provide an incentive for faculty to retire at age 62. The model used 15 states, with each of the first seven states being a year in rank for non-tenured faculty. Each of the remaining eight states reflected tenured faculty in age cohorts of five years, beginning at age 30 (state 8) and concluding with age 65 and

The key questions . . . must relate directly to the goals and objectives for which it is considering establishing the program.

older (state 15). The model used was a slightly modified version of a model described by Hopkins and Massy (1981, p. 343).

The purpose of the modeling was to project the age and tenure status of the faculty through the year 2000, assuming no changes were made in the annual turnover rate (recent five-year historical rates), and then to project a faculty profile to the year 2000 with the assumption that an incentive retirement program would induce a specified increased percentage of faculty to retire from state 14 (ages 60 to 64). The value of the modeling was that it permitted the program developers to make some judgments about the level of faculty participation that would be necessary to achieve the objectives for which the program was being developed (Chronister and Trainer 1985b, pp. 195–96).

Another strategy that has proven beneficial to decision makers in projecting characteristics of faculty over a period of time is the use of computer simulations. Simulators have the capability of modeling faculty cohorts on a year-by-year basis, using a random number generator to simulate the career path of individual faculty members in the simulation (Mortimer, Bagshaw, and Masland 1985). Simulators are most applicable to relatively small cohorts of faculty (200 to 250) because of the massive number of variables that are involved when dealing with individual faculty members, while Markov models use data on cohorts of faculty and defined probabilities about the cohorts of faculty in each state.

A computer simulation model was used at Colgate University to assess the effects of tenure and retirement policies on the institution's faculty (Nevison 1980). The institution was assessing two policy alternatives: the mandatory retirement age of 68 in effect at the time versus the new mandated age 70, and a change of tenure ratio from 55 percent to 65 percent. The purpose of the simulation was to assess the effects of those policy changes on the rate of tenuring, the tenure ratio, salary costs, and affirmative action (p. 159). The value of the use of simulation rather than a faculty flow model was the degree of precision and detail that the computer simulation provided in dealing with what was perceived to be an essential institutional policy decision.

Econometric simulations of the effects of retirement income and changes in retirement income on the retirement decision making of faculty are also beneficial to institutions attempting to estimate faculty retirement behavior regarding incentive early retirement programs (Weiler 1981, p. 130).

As an institution considers the use of models to assist with policy development, the model chosen must be the one that will provide the results necessary to assist policy makers in the decision that is to be made, but the decision makers must use sound judgment and experience in finally arriving at the planned course of action (Mortimer, Bagshaw, and Masland 1985, p. 70).

Cost/Benefit Considerations of Early Retirement Programs
After establishing the objectives for an incentive early retirement program and completing an analysis of the characteristics of the faculty to whom the program will be addressed, the development of the offering will rely heavily upon the costs and benefits of the options available (Chronister and Trainer 1985b, p. 200). The financial issues to be addressed will involve both faculty concerns and institutional constraints and capabilities.

The term "cost/benefit analysis," as used in the context of decision making for early retirement programs, is especially meaningful. Cost, as applied to faculty considering participating in an early retirement program, can involve the potential loss of salary derived from years of continued employment, a loss in the amount of retirement annuity as the result of a reduction in years of service (or additional contributions to the annuity pool), loss of university services, loss of medical benefits, et cetera. The benefits for faculty can be identified as the freedom from employment constraints that retirement provides as well as financial gains derived from the incentive program that is offered to faculty to retire early. These costs and benefits are an individual matter for faculty that a program must recognize.

In a similar manner, the costs and benefits for the institution must be defined. The costs will include factors other than purely financial ones, such as the loss of faculty members whom the institution might choose not to lose. The institutional benefits are the achievement of the objectives for which the program was established.

The faculty perspective

The factors that faculty have identified as being important in choosing an age at which to retire include projected retirement income in relation to estimated financial need, the potential impact of inflation on long-term retirement income, concerns about leaving the teaching profession and the institutional community, personal health, the cost of medical insurance after retirement, and loss of access to institutional services (Chronister and Trainer 1985b, p. 197; Palmer 1984).

Income during the early retirement years is an important consideration for faculty. Analysis of data from the 1977 Ladd-Lipset survey of college and university faculty indicates that among those aged 55 to 62, one-third would have considered early retirement if they were assured of income equal to one-half of their annual salary. The interest in early retirement increased to 40 percent of the survey sample if payment amounted to the full normal retirement annuity and to two-thirds if early retirement income equaled their current annual salary (Palmer and Patton 1978, p. 16). Another study, of the retirement plans of faculty of the University of California, identified a large early retirement annuity as a primary condition for early retirement (Patton 1977, p. 352).

A survey of all faculty aged 45 and over in the state of Oregon's higher education system in 1980 found that faculty would like to retire as much as three years earlier if conditions permitted (Mitchell 1981). Of those surveyed, 43 percent desired enhanced income for full retirement, 28 percent desired phased retirement, and 11 percent desired a 6 percent income supplement. The three most important conditions for encouraging early retirement were increased (retirement) income, continued health insurance coverage, and the option of part-time employment (p. 8). And a 1981 study conducted by TIAA found that 50 percent of the 1,438 respondents aged 59 to 69 expressed an interest in a phased retirement program (Mulanaphy 1981, p. 37).

The strategies for calculating the costs and benefits for faculty participating in an incentive early retirement program vary according to the objectives of such an analysis. Policy makers developing a program for faculty members must take into consideration individual faculty concerns as well as institutional interests and constraints.

TABLE 2

SAMPLE PROJECTION OF EARLY RETIREMENT INCOME[a]

	Year 1	Year 2	Year 3	Totals
Employment Income				
Gross salary	$35,000	$36,750	$38,590	$110,340
Less FICA and taxes	9,870	10,670	11,495	32,035
Net Salary	$25,130	$26,080	$27,095	$78,305
Retirement Income				
Social security income	$10,320	$10,733	$11,162	$32,215
Early retirement supplement	13,750	14,188	14,648	42,586
Less taxes	1,634	1,729	1,827	5,190
Net Income	$22,436	$23,192	$23,983	$69,611
Net Income as Percent of Net Salary	89.28	88.93	88.51	88.90
Difference in Net Income	$2,694	$2,888	$3,112	$8,694

[a]For a faculty member aged 62 with an annual salary of $35,000.

Source: Adapted from Chronister and Trainer 1985b, p. 201.

An example of such calculations for faculty is presented in table 2 (Chronister and Trainer 1985b, p. 201). These calculations were computed for a bridging program that used a combination of social security income and a monthly payment by the institution to bring early retirees' net income up to at least 75 percent of what the net income would have been had the faculty member remained in full employment at the institution. The program had a threshold age for eligibility of 62 and provided incentive benefits for three years, not to exceed age 65. It called for continued contributions to the faculty member's retirement annuity as though full-time employment had been maintained and continued participation in the institution's health insurance programs for the three years.

The institutional bridging payment was based upon a formula that consisted of multiplying the first $20,000 of salary by 50 percent and adding to it 25 percent of the gross salary over $20,000 of the last year of full employment. To accommodate concerns with the possible impact of inflation on the bridging payment, full-time salary for the last year was increased by 5 percent per year for the three years of early retirement to calculate the bridging payment. It is evident from the formula that the lower the faculty member's salary, the higher the percent net retirement income is when compared to the net income that would have been derived from full-time employment.

The social security benefit annuity was calculated for age 62 according to the early withdrawal penalty formula that reduces the annuity at age 65 by $\frac{1}{36} \times 20$ percent for each month of retirement before 65.

Thus, the goal of providing the faculty member with a net retirement income of at least 75 percent of the employment income, assuming annual salary increases of 5 percent, was achieved. When the formula is applied to a faculty member with an annual salary of $45,000, the net early retirement income as a percent of net salary income drops to an average 78 percent, or a drop in total net income for the three years of about $20,800 (Chronister and Trainer 1985b, p. 202).

Through analyses of data such as the one in table 2, faculty members have the opportunity to assess the financial significance of the decision to participate in early retirement programs. An additional projection that might be called for is a projection on what the retirement annuity will be for a faculty member when full retirement begins at age 65.

The example in table 2 is for an institution whose retirement plan is a defined contribution program; therefore, the continued retirement contributions during the three years of early retirement are important for two reasons. First, the continued contributions increase the annuity pool base through the additional contributions plus the fund's additional three years of investment earnings. In defined contribution programs, a reduction in the number of years of investment and earnings severely reduces the value of the retirement fund and therefore the retiree's ultimate annuity income.

Second, the three years of additional participation affect the actuarial projections used to arrive at the annual annuity income for the faculty member by reducing the actuarially derived number of years of payout.

In summary, the following statement should be considered by all institutions planning to offer such a program.

An employee who retires early is foregoing his years of peak earning capacity. Further, a retired professor must have more than mere economic security; in retirement he must not be forced to abandon entirely the twin sources of his professional self-esteem: his students and his studies (Gross 1977b, p. 754).

The 1980 Statement of Principles on Academic Retirement and Insurance Plans of the American Association of University Professors underscores the need to consider professional self-esteem (AAUP 1980, p. 323). Institutions can provide benefits to help offset the "professional costs" of early retirement: "a mail address, library privileges, office facilities, faculty club membership, the institution's publications, secretarial help, administration of grants, laboratory rights, faculty dining privileges, and participation in convocations and academic processions" (AAUP 1980, p. 323).

The institutional perspective

Assuming that an institution is planning to use a "formal" incentive early retirement plan to achieve some stated objectives, it must recognize and be prepared to deal with two important cost/benefit considerations:

1. Will it lose some of its "best" faculty (faculty the institution would choose to retain)?
2. How much will the program cost in institutional dollars?

Institutions must recognize that an incentive plan can be structured to discourage participation by faculty the institution desires to retain. And ample literature suggests that the more productive faculty do not seek early retirement. Two studies are particularly relevant to the concerns about the loss of an institution's "best" faculty.

In one study, the individuals most interested in incentive early retirement plans of any kind tended to be those who judged their performance as below that of their colleagues (Patton 1983a). And a survey of 1,200 tenured faculty in the public colleges and universities of Oregon found that a strong positive association existed between faculty expressing unhappiness with their current work and those who indicated the possibility of accepting early retirement incentives. Overall, early retirement incentive programs do not disproportionately deplete institutions of their better teachers (Toevs and Handhardt 1982).

. The second important element in the decision about the use of an incentive early retirement program and the option selected is the program's financial impact on the institution. That impact can also be approached from several perspectives.

The material in table 2 contains information useful in assessing the impact of that program on the institution. For the faculty member aged 62 at $35,000 salary, the total costs of employment compensation would amount to approximately $139,500, whereas the early retirement incentive costs, including benefits, would amount to about $63,400 (Chronister and Trainer 1985b, p. 201). From a financial perspective, the program met its objective. It provided funds that could be used to hire replacement faculty, one of the stated objectives for the program (p. 202).

A Generic Cost Analysis Formula
The following generic formula can be modified to evaluate options for an incentive early retirement program (Kepple 1984, p. 57). To use the formula, an institution must provide some basic information and make some assumptions.

First, the institution should establish the salary or average salary of those faculty who are expected to retire. In the following example, the 1982–83 AAUP II.B. average salary for professor rank is adjusted upward slightly to reflect the expectation that retiring faculty are higher paid than the average professor.

Second, the institution should establish the average number of years that faculty are expected to retire earlier under the program. In the example, three years earlier is used. A number of studies (Kepple 1984; Mitchell 1981, for example) indicate that three years is a very likely average result, although most faculty will retire a year or two earlier and a few up to five or ten years earlier.

Third, the institution should project the expected average salary of incoming faculty if all or some of the vacated places will be filled. The example uses the 1982–83 AAUP II.B. average salary for assistant rank.

Fourth, the institution must include fringe benefits affected by retirement and/or by waiting periods.

Two primary factors should be included in the fringe benefit cost analysis:

1. *Health insurance.* In some cases, institutions continue health insurance into retirement at institutional expense. If a replacement faculty member is hired, however, health insurance costs could as much as double.
2. *Contributions to the retirement plan.* Except in incentive early retirement programs that continue college contributions to a retiring faculty member's retirement program, college contributions cease at retirement.

In the generic formula, these factors have not been included because they vary so widely among institutions.

Fifth, the institution must project the expected salary increases over the period of early retirement. Salaries are adjusted upward by 5 percent per year in the example.

To provide the most accurate estimate of current savings and costs, the sample uses a 10 percent present value factor. The present value factor adjusts for the fact that a dollar today is worth more to a college than a dollar a year from today. For example, a college can use lump-sum payments up front to encourage early retirements, assuming that it will obtain future savings in salaries, but a current lump-sum payment is worth more than future dollars saved in salaries. Any future incentive payments, such as bridging payments, must also be discounted to their present value.

The resulting formula for generic salary with an incentive early retirement program is as follows:

Year	Salary Saved		Present Value Factor		Amount
1	$31,736	×	.9545	=	$30,292
2	33,323	×	.8675	=	28,907
3	34,989	×	.7885	=	27,588
Estimated Present Value of Salary Saved					$86,787

These savings will be reduced by the estimated cost of the

incentive. In many cases, the college might plan to replace some or all of the vacated positions with new faculty; therefore, the following generic replacement faculty salary formula can be used:

Year	Salary		Present Value Factor		Amount
1	$20,632	×	.9545	=	$19,693
2	21,664	×	.8675	=	18,793
3	22,747	×	.7885	=	17,936
Estimated Present Value of Salary Expense					**$56,422**

By comparing the cost of the incentive and the replacement faculty salary to the salary saved by the retirement and projecting the number of retirements, a financial analysis of the incentive early retirement program can be established. The following example illustrates the application of the formula.

College A plans to offer a lump-sum incentive program. It expects 10 faculty members to accept early retirement at an average lump-sum payment of $47,000 each. Three of the faculty members will be replaced with new assistant professors at a starting salary of $20,632, and one will be replaced at an associate professor's salary of $41,264. Thus:

10 faculty × $86,787 in salary savings each = $867,870 in total salary savings

10 incentives at $47,000 each = $470,000 in incentive costs

3 assistant professors at $56,422 each (including compensation costs) and 1 associate professor at $112,844 = $282,110 in new salary expenses

The expected saving generated by this incentive program equals $115,760 ($867,870 − $470,000 − $282,110 = $115,760).

Many institutions expect to lose money on an incentive early retirement program because the institutional objective for the program is to replace many or all of the vacated positions (Kepple 1984, p. 139). If College A replaces each retired faculty member with a new assistant professor, the additional cost of the program would be \$166,350 [\$867,870 − \$470,000 − (10 × \$56,422) = −\$166,350].

Thus, it is important for an institution to adequately assess the purpose of its incentive program and the financial resources that can be committed to such an endeavor.

The Legal Perspective
The following observation is sound advice for any institution formulating an incentive early retirement program.

> *An early or phased retirement plan may be affected by current social security law, the Employee Retirement Income Security Act, or by state and local law. . . . No plan can actually serve as a complete model for another institution. If a college or university chooses to develop an early retirement plan, it should do so only after consulting legal counsel* (Covert-McGrath 1984a, p. 13).

The use of legal counsel in the development of incentive early retirement programs is clearly important in a period of changing tax and social legislation to ensure compliance with state and federal laws and regulations (Clevenger and Chronister 1986, p. 10).

INSTITUTIONAL EXPERIENCES WITH
EARLY RETIREMENT PROGRAMS

In view of the growth of incentive early retirement programs offered by institutions of higher education, important lessons are to be learned from the experiences of those colleges and universities. In 1981, early retirement programs were much talked about, but little solid empirical published work existed (Mitchell 1981, p. 2). Since then, a number of studies have been undertaken to fill that void. This section presents the findings of several studies of systems of institutions as well as studies of the experiences of individual colleges and universities that offer incentive early retirement programs. It includes the types of programs offered and how well the programs have been meeting the institutions' objectives and purposes for which they were established.

The most common types of programs offered were severance payments, bridging payments, and phased retirement.

Early Retirement Program Incentives Offered
Approximately 35 percent of the 318 institutions that responded to the Project on Reallocation Study provided incentives for faculty to retire early (Mortimer, Bagshaw, and Masland 1985). By institutional type, 55 percent of the doctoral-degree-granting institutions, 45 percent of the comprehensive colleges and universities, and 23 percent of the liberal arts colleges reported the provision of incentives. Public institutions were more likely to have formalized early retirement programs than were private colleges and universities. Among the types of incentives provided by the institutions, approximately 8 percent offered reduced teaching loads, about 13 percent provided continued employee benefits after retirement, about 15 percent offered supplemental retirement income, and approximately 49 percent offered a combination of incentives (p. 45).

A study of incentive early retirement programs in private liberal arts colleges identified 39 colleges with plans (Kepple 1984). Seventy-four percent of the institutions classified their programs as formal offerings, 17.9 percent identified them as informal or individually negotiated options, and the remaining 7.7 percent indicated they provided both formal and informal options to faculty interested in retiring early (p. 152). The most common types of programs offered were severance payments (used by 25.6 percent of the colleges), bridging payments (20.5 percent), and phased retirement (12.8 percent). A substantial 20.5 percent offered two or more options for faculty members' choice, and nearly 12.8 percent of the colleges indicated that anything was negotiable.

The use of combinations of incentives to meet the interests and needs of faculty candidates for early retirement appears to be a common practice (Chronister and Trainer 1985a; Kepple 1984; Mortimer, Bagshaw, and Masland 1985). Among 51 institutions responding to a 1984 survey of early, partial, and phased retirement programs in public universities, 45 percent (23 institutions) offered a single program option to faculty. A full early retirement option, offered by 13 institutions, was the most popular; six institutions offered a partial retirement option, and four offered phased retirement (Chronister and Trainer 1985a, p. 28). Among the nearly 55 percent reporting that they offered combinations of program options, the most common combination (reported by 11 institutions) involved providing for early retirement with partial reemployment as an incentive in the program. Within the cohort of institutions offering multiple programs, a number of the institutions indicated that the full early retirement program and a partial or phased program were in fact separate opportunities for faculty.

A number of formal early retirement programs offered by state institutions with defined benefit retirement plans provide credit for additional years of service. Faculty and other employees of California state university and colleges who, at the time of retirement, were age 50 or older and had five or more years of service credit in the Public Employees' Retirement System or the State Teachers' Retirement System were awarded two years of unearned service credit toward their retirement annuities if they retired during a defined period of eligibility (Reinhard 1981, p. 12). In a similar vein, faculty and other employees of the State University of New York and the City University of New York who met certain criteria for eligibility were offered an early retirement option that included three years of unearned service credit in the calculation of their retirement annuity (Ingalls 1985).

Providing part-time employment as a component of an early retirement program often meets the desire of faculty to continue contact with students and colleagues or to provide a measure of economic security and can therefore be viewed as an important elective incentive. Part-time employment can also be a legal requirement in an incentive early retirement program for public institutions so that the program complies with state statutes. Analysis of the program in a public university in the state of Washington indicated that because state statutes prohibited any payments of state funds except for services rendered, part-time employment was a necessary part of the incentive early retirement program for the institution (Clevenger and Chronister 1986, p. 41). In Washington, therefore, public institutions that offer formal early retirement programs guarantee part-time employment for a specified number of years to those faculty who desire to avail themselves of this economic aspect of the incentive program.

For public institutions in Ohio, state statutes preclude the guarantee of part-time employment as a component of an early retirement program. Therefore, such employment is only a possibility and at the discretion and convenience of the institution (Clevenger and Chronister 1986, p. 41).

Although many institutions provide for part-time employment of faculty in their incentive early retirement programs, Oakland University in Michigan provides an interesting contrast. The 1983–85 collective bargaining agreement between Oakland University and its local chapter of AAUP included a provision for the university to reemploy any retired bargaining unit faculty member, with the exception of those who had participated in the institution's voluntary early retirement option (AAUP 1983, p. 59).

Incentives vary widely (Kepple 1984). Model College 1 in Kepple's study provided a lump-sum payment equal to the scheduled faculty salary for the current year minus the beginning salary for an assistant professor for the same year. To be eligible to participate in the incentive program, a faculty member had to be between ages 55 and 64 and have been employed by the institution for at least 10 years (p. 83). Model 4 in Kepple's study provided a year's paid leave of absence and a contribution to the individual faculty member's retirement plan based upon a formula ranging from 180 percent of the previous year's annuity contribution at age 65 to 20 percent at age 69 (p. 92).

Model 7 provided phased employment for faculty members at age 62 with 10 years of employment. Teaching load and salary were reduced to 50 percent of the level of the previous year. In addition, the college continued contributions to the retiree's retirement plan based on 15 percent of the prior full-time salary, escalating at the rate of average annual salary increases (Kepple 1984, p. 102). Model College 8 provided a "bridging benefit" payment equal to 10 percent of the individual faculty member's prior year salary. To be eligible, the individual must have had 10 years of continuous service to the college and be 62. The bridging payment continues until age 65 (p. 106).

Another incentive is a preretirement supplement plan. The college provides the faculty who agree to retire at age 65 or before up to 7.5 percent additional matching supplement to the individual's current retirement contribution. The supplement can begin at age 55 or whenever the agreement is signed between the ages of 55 and 65. In addition, the college pays half salary to the retiree for the year following retirement (Kepple 1984, p. 126).

Effectiveness of Program Offerings:
The Institutional Perspective

The effectiveness of incentive early retirement programs is an issue that must be addressed as institutions seek to determine strategies for meeting demands for flexible staffing. To provide a baseline for assessing effectiveness of the programs at the 51 institutions in one study, the respondents were requested to identify, from a prepared list, those objectives that served as the reasons for the development of the incentive program(s) at their institutions (Chronister and Trainer 1985a). "To provide a faculty benefit" was cited for nearly 40 percent of the programs, "to create financial savings" for about 18 percent, "to provide for reallocation of resources" for about 16 percent, "to provide for renewal of the professoriate" for 13 percent, and "to reduce the tenure ratio" for about 10 percent; about 3 percent cited other reasons. Interpreted another way, approximately 60 percent of the responses cited program purposes that can be classified as beneficial to the institution. This finding strongly supports the contention that incentive early retirement programs for faculty are strategies that provide institutions of higher education with a means of managing faculty resources.

Another finding of the study of the 51 institutions was that only four of them had established actual numerical goals for faculty positions to be vacated through offering early, partial, and/or phased retirement programs, and only four programs had established targets for dollars saved (Chronister and Trainer 1985a, p. 29). Although no explicit numerical goals had been established for the vast majority of the programs, institutions overwhelmingly asserted that the programs were achieving the purposes for which they had been established. When success of the programs was viewed from the perspective of the level of faculty participation, 80 percent of the early retirement programs were cited as having achieved participation at or above the expected level. The vast majority of the institutions offering those program options also reported that participation in the partial and phased programs was at or above the expected levels (p. 30).

The Kepple study of early retirement programs at liberal arts colleges found that the 39 college presidents rated the programs as generally successful in terms of meeting their expectations of faculty participation. Specifically, 7.7 percent stated that the faculty reception exceeded expectations, 41 percent characterized the program as matching expectations, 5.1 percent indicated a failure to match expectations, and 46.2 percent stated that their program had not been in existence long enough to assess its effectiveness (Kepple 1984, p. 79).

An analysis of the California state university and colleges' early retirement program also provides evidence of the potential attractiveness of formalized programs in meeting institutional needs to reduce faculty staffing. The California program, established in anticipation of the need to reduce staff, provided an incentive bonus of two years of unearned retirement service credit in the calculation of the retirement annuity for eligible staff members who availed themselves of the program. The majority of those who retired under the program indicated that the two years service credit was a major factor in their decision to retire early. This program, which was offered only for a three-month enrollment period in 1980, was also found to be financially beneficial to the institutions because the cost of funding the two years of unearned service credit for retirement purposes was less costly than the anticipated compensation costs for the faculty had they not chosen to retire early (Reinhard 1981, p. 68).

An incentive early retirement program established for employees of state-supported colleges and universities in

New York encouraged a large number of early retirements (Ingalls 1985). The New York program provided an extra three years of service credit for participants that increased an individual's pension payment by about 5 percent per year. In terms of the number of employees who took advantage of the program, it can be described as successful, although some effects can be cited as negative. The fact that more than 20 percent of the eligible staff took advantage of the option at one time created a concern for several of the campus administrators.

Michigan State University used a severance pay incentive plan to encourage early retirement among faculty whose positions were subject to termination notice because of a declared financial crisis at the institution in 1981. The "buyout" incentive was offered only to "potentially affected" faculty members and can therefore be viewed as providing a positive (or voluntary) action by faculty as opposed to a negative dismissal action by the institution. The plan had two variations: (1) a complete buyout with payment of up to two years of salary for faculty in certain programs, and (2) a partial buyout or part-time employment option for faculty in other targeted program areas. Through this induced early retirement program, Michigan State achieved the desired reduction of approximately 100 targeted faculty positions (Kreinin 1982, p. 37).

While Michigan State University's incentive plan was developed during the turmoil following a declaration of financial crisis by the institution's board of trustees and the announcement of plans to terminate 100 tenured and eight tenure-stream faculty (Kreinin 1982, p. 37), Adelphi University provided an early retirement plan that appears to have the support of faculty (Heller 1984, p. 17). Adelphi's plan provided three options, the most popular of which involved faculty whose age and years of teaching service added to 65 or over. Faculty meeting that criterion and choosing to retire early receive a percentage of their salary, decreasing annually over five years, as well as full benefits. Other options include the "repurchase" of a tenured contract and a three-year unpaid leave of absence. Twenty-eight faculty members participated in the program the first year, with the majority taking the full early retirement option. Sixteen faculty signed up for the program the second year (p. 17).

Rhodes College in Memphis, Tennessee, offered a limited-term incentive early retirement program that has proven to be highly successful in meeting institutional needs (American Council on Education 1986). Faced with a tenure rate of about 87 percent in 1981 that restricted the flexibility the college felt it needed to plan effectively for the 1980s and 1990s, the institution, with significant input from faculty, developed a dual option program. One option provided faculty members who were age 62 or younger with a severance payment of 150 percent of salary. The percentage of salary for the severance payment declined as the age of the faculty member choosing early retirement increased. The other option was phased retirement that permitted the faculty to retire but to continue teaching for up to 40 percent of a normal load.

Rhodes College's program was introduced in January 1983 and provided for a five-month enrollment window during which faculty could contract for immediate or deferred early retirement. As a result of the offering, by December 1985 a total of seven faculty members had retired early under the severance pay option, and another nine contracted for early retirement between 1986 and 1995. When these retirements are added to the nine faculty members who are scheduled for mandatory retirement by 1995, 30 percent of the college's total faculty will have retired in a 12-year period.

A number of institutions have developed early retirement programs with the dual objectives of increasing flexibility in staffing while at the same time seeking to reduce staff. A university in the northeast implemented an incentive program with these twin objectives and has classified the program a success (Clevenger and Chronister 1986, pp. 10–18). Adopted in 1982 and established for a five-year enrollment period, the program provides incentive payments for faculty members between the ages of 62 and 69 with 10 years of service who retire early. Faculty closest to age 62 receive the highest incentive payments, with the amount of the payment reduced the closer to age 69 the faculty member chooses to retire.

The institution has reported a participation rate higher than initially expected but not at a level deemed disadvantageous to the university. Whereas approximately 10 percent of eligible faculty retired early the year before implementation of the program, the rate increased to 29, 21, and 25 percent during the first three years of the incentive offerings (Clevenger and Chronister 1986, p. 16). These participation rates have permitted the university to create some financial savings by reducing staff while at the same time reallocating a limited number of entry-level positions.

The opportunity for partial employment as the basis of an early retirement program is an important consideration for many faculty contemplating retirement. Although many institutions offer such an option to prospective early retirees, the requirement of partial employment in one institutional program has not been a deterrent to faculty. An institution in the northwest has a requirement of partial employment as the basis for its early retirement program because of state regulations. The program, which has a threshold age for eligibility of 62, was implemented in 1980 and has averaged 25 participants per year, except for 1982–83, when the state offered a six-month period when the age for eligibility was reduced to 55. During that year, a total of 110 faculty members availed themselves of the opportunity to retire early (Clevenger and Chronister 1986, pp. 19–25).

Although faculty members are eligible for reemployment at a 40 percent effort and salary level until age 70, actual faculty participation in reemployment drops to less than 20 to 30 percent of faculty retirees after their third year of early retirement. The only drawback to the program from the perspective of the institution is that the institution has lost a number of faculty considered outstanding scholars that the institution would rather not have lost (Clevenger and Chronister 1986, p. 24).

A number of systemwide incentive early retirement programs have been authorized by state legislatures to lower employment levels in the affected agencies. This situation was the case in 1982 in the state of Washington when Second Substitute House Bill 124 was passed. According to the preamble of the bill:

> *The legislature has determined it is in the best interest of the state to temporarily provide for a special early retirement benefit which would enable certain employees to leave state service. It is the intent of the legislature that the lower level of employment achieved through the utilization of this special early retirement be maintained by*

the agency or political subdivision by whom the retiring employee was employed (Carbone 1983, p. 1).

Under the incentive early retirement plan developed for higher education personnel within the state system, college and university employees who were members of the teachers' retirement system or the public employees' retirement system who had five years of service credit and were age 55 could retire under the program; if they had 25 years of service, they could retire at any age. Members who were participants in the TIAA/CREF retirement plan could retire regardless of age if they had 25 years of service; if they were 55 years of age with 10 years of service in TIAA/CREF, they were eligible to retire under the incentive plan (Carbone 1983, p. 2). Employees who met these requirements were given an eight-month enrollment period during which they could enroll in the program (p. 1).

A study of the impact of the special retirement program on community college personnel compared data on early and regular retirees during the period when the early retirement option was made available to staff. The program was available to all eligible community college staff; 85 staff members took advantage of the offering, of whom 37 (43.5 percent) were faculty members. During the same period, 159 other employees retired under the regular retirement plan, 73 (45.9 percent) of whom were faculty members (Carbone 1983, p. 4). Based upon the goals of the special retirement program as set forth in the preamble to the legislation, the program was deemed a success from the perspective of reducing staff. The assessment of the financial implications of the program is a bit less sanguine. Compensation savings from faculty early retirements were more likely to result in cost reductions for the system because of the tendency within the colleges to replace full-time retirees with part-time personnel (p. 3). The longer-term costs to the state may offset these immediate savings because of the payment of pension benefits to the early retirees for a longer period of time. This factor is especially applicable to nonfaculty personnel, who tend to retire at the earliest possible opportunity, an opportunity provided by the special program (p. 4).

Against this backdrop of generally favorable assessments of the effectiveness of early retirement programs, it must be

The opportunity for partial employment as the basis of an early retirement program is an important consideration for many faculty contemplating retirement.

---

recognized that some professionals find few of the programs successful (Palmer 1984, p. 23), although many other studies do not support this observation (Chronister and Trainer 1985a; Clevenger and Chronister 1986; Kepple 1984).

Effectiveness of Programs: The Faculty Perspective
If participation is the criterion for the effectiveness of early retirement programs, the programs described in the preceding section could be inferred to be effective from the perspective of individual faculty members. The effectiveness of such programs, as viewed from faculty members' perspective, however, has not been the subject of a significant amount of research. The effectiveness of the programs for faculty members relates to more than pure economics, although economics is a fundamental consideration (Palmer 1984, p. 23).

A 1977 study of early retirees from four universities found that 93 percent of the 42 retirees who were interviewed indicated that they were satisfied, or very satisfied, with their decision (Kell and Patton 1978, p. 175). Eighty-eight percent of the retirees reported that they were well off financially. Further, a majority of the respondents had remained professionally active after retirement, and 71 percent had been employed at one time or another during retirement (p. 176). And 90 percent of the retired faculty members interviewed would make the same decision again; 81 percent felt very satisfied with the provisions of the early retirement program offered by their institutions.

The potential negative impact of early retirement on the retirement annuity is a reason that a number of faculty members choose not to participate in incentive early retirement programs. Unless the early retirement program incentives include a provision for offsetting the financial loss of reduced annuity payments, faculty in defined contribution retirement programs, such as TIAA/CREF, will face severely reduced annuity payments. A faculty member at Muhlenberg College in Pennsylvania figured that if he took advantage of the program offered by that institution at age 60, he would receive $100,000 from the college over five years and $9,600 annually for 20 years from TIAA/CREF, whereas if he worked until age 65, the annuity would be about $20,000 per year for 20 years (Palmer 1984, p. 24). The potential decrease in the amount of retirement annuity income is a critical concern for many potential early retirees; it is in fact one of the variables that has been cited as a deterrent to participation in such programs.

Another expressed deterrent to participation in early retirement programs for a number of eligible faculty members is the loss of contact with students. As one such eligible faculty member stated, "My students keep me alive. It would be a deprivation not to see them" (Palmer 1984, p. 23). This statement reflects one of the reasons that a number of incentive programs provide for partial employment as an option. Such an option provides faculty with both an economic and a professional incentive for participation.

Actual and Potential Problems in
Incentive Retirement Programs
The potential loss of distinguished faculty who probably would not be lost in the absence of the incentive program is an issue that institutions contemplating offering early retirement programs must consider. With an incentive program that must leave the option of participation in the program to faculty's prerogative, it is very difficult for an institution to target the faculty it wants to take advantage of the program. One effect of the New York program was the reported loss of a number of distinguished faculty members who were considered the strengths of their departments (Ingalls 1985).

At one institution, the early retirement program permits the institution to delay the early retirement of a faculty member for up to 12 months, at no loss of benefits to the individual, if it is in the interest of the university (Clevenger and Chronister 1986, p. 12). Many incentive programs include program statements that provide, "in the interest of the institution," the right to defer faculty members' participation for a period of time or the right to participate at all.

The faculty early retirement incentive plan that is included as part of the collective bargaining agreement at Marymount College in Tarrytown, New York, includes two statements in the section dealing with eligibility for participation that are especially specific in setting forth the institution's interests.

4-2 A Faculty Member's participation in the Plan must result in a net savings to the College during the Incentive Payment Period.

4-3 Eligible Faculty Members may elect to participate in the Plan and the option to initiate the election rests solely with the Faculty Member. However, notwithstanding anything to the contrary contained in the Plan, the College has the absolute right to reject that election; the College's rejection shall be final and unreviewable, and shall not be subject to any of the grievance or arbitration provisions contained in the collective bargaining agreement (AAUP 1984, p. 35).

These statements very clearly set forth the fact that the institution retains the right to choose those who participate from among those who are eligible and those who apply to participate. It is further specified in section 4-7, which refers to the fact that ". . . no employee of the College shall become a participant unless he or she is one of a select group of management or highly compensated employees of the College" (p. 36). The agreement further reserves the right for the college to delay implementation of a faculty member's entry into the program for one year after the individual has been approved for participation (p. 36).

The voluntary nature of such programs for faculty is a requirement that is dictated by the Age Discrimination in Employment Act. It has been possible, however, for institutions to target certain populations of faculty as eligible for early retirement without violating regulations governing equity and fairness.

The targeting of populations of faculty as eligible for participation in an early retirement program is possible when such targeting is consistent with institutional objectives and ADEA and when the option to participate resides with the select faculty cohort. One institution used a priority system to specify the departments in which the need was greatest to reduce staff. The priority system was designed to give highest priority to interested faculty who were in the most overstaffed departments. Within the funding cap established to support the incentives set forth for the program, if more faculty applied for the program than the budget could support, the faculty were to be ranked by means of a weighting system related directly to the degree of overstaffing in the departments. The higher the degree of overstaffing of the department in which a faculty member taught, the greater the possibility of early retirement for faculty members from that unit. Since the implementation of this program, beginning with the 1983–84 academic year, the priority system had been invoked in only one year because, except for that year, the number of applicants for the program has not exceeded the funding cap (Clevenger and Chronister 1986, pp. 27–34).

The program offered by Michigan State University in 1981–82 can be classified as a targeted incentive plan because the incentives were offered to faculty whose positions were subject to termination because they were members of schools or academic programs that were subject to elimination (Kreinin 1982, p. 37).

A second type of targeting evident in institutional plans involves designating faculty members in certain age groups as desirable candidates for early retirement and building incentives so that retirement before or after the target age is financially less attractive (Clevenger and Chronister 1986). One institution calculates the amount of the early retirement incentive payment based upon a scale that uses factors consisting of the number of years of service and the age at early retirement. The maximum incentive payment a faculty member can collect is 50 percent of his or her last annual salary before early retirement. For example, a faculty member choosing to retire at age 62 with 25 years of service would receive the maximum incentive. If the retirement is delayed until age 65, the maximum payment would be reduced to 41 percent, because the incentive payment declines by 3 percent per year beyond the threshold age of 62. The payment also declines as the number of years of service declines. This particular institution appears to be satisfied with the program, noting that 83 faculty members had chosen to participate during the first three years it was offered. When viewed from the perspective of participation by eligible faculty, the rate varied from 21 and 29 percent per year across the three years (p. 16).

Institutions also have the option in their program offerings to open a "window" for faculty participation that is constrained to a specific age and a period of time during which faculty must choose to enroll in the program or forfeit the right to participate. As an example, the State University System's early retirement program provided by the Board of Regents in Florida, which was in effect from 1983 to 1985, included such a stipulation (Turnbull 1986). Faculty who had accrued at least 10 years of creditable service and who were 62 years of age or older during the 1984–85 year were required to enroll in the program before May 31, 1985, or forfeit the right to future participation. Such a stipulation does not require participation in an incentive early retirement program but does set institutional (or state) parameters for those faculty who do choose to participate. The Florida program provided half-time employment for faculty as one of the benefits.

A program developed in 1980 to assist an institution with a goal of reallocating resources has proven to be successful (Clevenger and Chronister 1986, p. 19). The program, which uses part-time employment as one of its incentives because of state restrictions on payments that can be made to faculty, has had an average of 25 faculty participate each year, with the exception of one year. That participation rate has been higher than expected. The program provides for early retirement beginning at age 62 with a reemployment option for up to 40 percent time until age 70. Individuals participating in the program have, on average, been retiring at age 64 or 65 (Clevenger and Chronister 1986, p. 23).

Program Modifications
In view of the dynamic nature of institutions of higher education and the changing environment in which they function, constant review of policies that affect personnel seems appropriate and necessary. Although the majority of programs discussed in the study of early, partial, and phased retirement programs in public higher education (Chronister and Trainer 1985a) had been established since about the time of the effective date of the amendments to ADEA (July 1, 1982), many of the programs had been adjusted subsequent to their initial implementation. Eleven early retirement, 10 partial retirement, and seven phased retirement programs had been adjusted, with the stated purpose of making them more attractive to faculty and/or to address a new institutional objective.

A common modification involved changing the age at which a faculty member is eligible to participate: Age 55 was most commonly identified as the new threshold. In several instances, this age became a permanent adjustment, but in one instance an institution's plan was changed for one year only to age 55 by state action, from which the

institution reaped a windfall number of early retirements
(see also Clevenger and Chronister 1986, p. 19). Another
frequently cited adjustment is to use years of service plus
age as a criterion in the determination of eligibility.

In keeping with the need to make programs more attractive to faculty, changes to partial and phased retirement
programs include such actions as making employment
options more flexible and increasing the income that can be
earned. One institution that based the half-time salary on
the average of the salary for the last three years modified
the percentage from 50 percent to 60 percent as a means of
having it more closely approximate one-half of the last
year's salary. Another adjustment a number of institutions
adopted was to lower the age at which a faculty member
could begin to participate in the program. Each modification can be viewed as benefiting faculty.

Two institutions participating in another study cited
changes to their partial and phased retirement programs that
were designed to increase institutional benefits. In both
cases, it involved reducing the number of years a faculty
member could be employed. The intent, as specified by one
respondent, was to promote the earlier appointment of new
faculty members (Chronister and Trainer 1985a, p. 31).

Institutions that provide incentive early retirement
opportunities for faculty on an ongoing basis will also need
to monitor the programs on a continuing basis. This contin-
ual monitoring and assessment should be a function of the
institution's desire to ascertain whether the program is
meeting the purposes for which it was established.
Changes in institutional circumstances and environmental
changes that might affect faculty decisions can necessitate
changes in program incentives—or even the advisability of
continuing to offer the program. A number of institutions
specify a required review of a program at selected times
and the establishment of a program for a defined number of
years (Chronister and Trainer 1985b; Clevenger and Chronister 1986).

CONCLUSIONS AND RECOMMENDATIONS

In 1974, the then-current literature on incentive early retirement programs "seem[ed] to create the impression, if not the illusion, that widespread application of early retirement plans is professionally essential, personally urgent, educationally desirable, and financially feasible" (Jenny 1974, p. 7). In the years since then, evidence has continued to build in support of the use of incentive early retirement programs to meet a number of higher education's faculty staffing and financial problems.

Clearly, incentive early retirement programs have become increasingly popular on college and university campuses as management tools to assist in dealing with problems of overstaffing, financial constraints, high tenure rates, the need to reallocate resources, the inability to hire new staff, and the inability to respond to students' changing curricular preferences.

Both institutions and early retirees generally favorably evaluate their incentive programs. It is still uncertain what impact these programs will have on higher education as a whole, but it is certain that properly structured programs can and have dramatically affected the staffing patterns at individual institutions. Incentive early retirement programs cannot be dismissed lightly as a passing fad, nor should they be viewed as a continuing resolution to management's poor decision making.

It is quite clear that incentive early retirement programs are shaped and controlled by federal statutes and regulations dealing with age discrimination, protection of retirement income for employees, and IRS stipulations on taxable income; therefore, any institution planning to develop an incentive program to facilitate early retirement of faculty and staff must be aware of such guidelines and restrictions. To these regulations must be added relevant state statutes regarding retirement and the use of state funds in support of benefits by public institutions.

Although this monograph reports a number of generally positive institutional experiences about the effectiveness of such programs, a number of cautions are in order. First, to a large degree, the success of an incentive program designed to facilitate the early retirement of faculty is a function of the problem the program is designed to alleviate, the age structure of the faculty to whom it is addressed, the nature of the incentives provided to faculty, and external social and eco-

It is certain that properly structured programs can and have dramatically affected the staffing patterns at individual institutions.

nomic variables that affect faculty decisions. The nature of the program is a function of the culture of the campus. Failure to recognize this observation will reduce the program's potential effectiveness.

Second, the literature suggests several steps that institutions should take to assist faculty in planning for retirement. The goal of retirement preparation programs is to ease the adjustment to life without work (Cox and Russell 1982, p. 1), but retirement for academics does not necessarily involve terminating their role, as faculty have the ability to pursue the same interests and style of life after retirement (p. 7). The desire of many faculty who are candidates for early retirement to retain an affiliation with the college or university after retirement is one factor that creates the need to provide continued institutional services as incentives in formal early retirement programs.

An effective *planning* program for faculty and staff is important to the success of early retirement programs. Preretirement counseling not only encourages senior faculty to consider the financial and personal options at retirement but also encourages younger faculty to prepare adequately for that future decision (Kepple 1984, p. 166).

And attention should be given to the person selected to administer the program. An individual who has the trust and respect of the faculty is much more likely to successfully negotiate and explain the options available.

Third, incentive early retirement programs do not necessarily pay for themselves. Programs under which each retiring faculty member is immediately replaced have difficulty generating savings in salary and fringe benefits in an amount equivalent to the amount necessary to also cover costs of the incentive plan. The fact that many institutions are using incentive early retirement programs to increase academic quality and flexibility rather than to reduce costs has implications for the cost effectiveness of such offerings.

It is also important to use strategies to develop and assess alternative approaches to dealing with the institutional problems that will provide decision makers with the best resolution of those problems. Incentive early retirement programs are not a panacea and may not be the best long-term resolution. The provision of incentives for faculty to retire early is a short-term strategy for reducing tenure ratios only if the distribution of faculty age is such that the incentive program addresses that issue (Hopkins 1972). An incentive program does not resolve a continuing problem of poor decision making about personnel appointments and retention: More cost-effective means are available to address such problems. If high tenure ratios are the cause of a problem, then the tenure process itself should be studied.

Early retirement programs are viewed as a fair and humane way to terminate faculty, but they are neither fair nor humane if they do not address faculty members' economic, professional, and personal concerns (Gross 1977b, p. 754). A critical concern for those faculty considering taking retirement before a regularly established retirement age or the mandatory age is protecting and maintaining the value of income after retirement, that is, maintaining an acceptable standard of living over the entire retirement period. This criterion involves not only establishing an adequate initial benefit but also protecting the benefit against the effects of inflation (Commission on College Retirement 1986, p. 12).

Although formal incentive early retirement programs have existed on college and university campuses for several decades, increased impetus in support of their development was provided by the 1978 amendments to ADEA, which raised the age of protected employees from 65 to 70. Passage of the 1986 amendments to ADEA abolished mandatory retirement by reason of age. Although the amendments provide higher education with a seven-year exemption to the uncapping of retirement for tenured faculty, the exemption is repealed at about the time when colleges and universities face their most crucial staffing problems.

A number of factors that colleges and universities are just now beginning to address have become increasingly significant. When the 1978 amendments were passed, higher education was given an exemption for four years to develop programs to accommodate the effects of tenure systems on staffing and retirement patterns. The most significant change that has taken place since then has been the growth in the number of institutions offering incentive early retirement programs. Interest has also increased in the development of post-tenure evaluation of faculty as a means of removing nonproductive and incompetent faculty (Licata 1986, p. 15).

An increased impetus for further development of programs for post-tenure review and incentive early retirement programs can be expected as a result of the uncapping of retirement by reason of age. The development of incentive retirement programs will be shaped extensively by the recent Tax Reform Act and by sections included in the Omnibus Budget Reconciliation Act of 1986.

It is interesting to note that although higher education was given a four-year exception to the 1978 amendments, approximately 85 percent of TIAA/CREF institutions did not invoke the exception that permitted them to retain a retirement age earlier than 70 (Calvin 1984, p. 4). Even though the institutions did not invoke the exception, the average age (65) of retirees did not increase significantly (p. 4).

Whether the abolition of mandatory retirement will engender the same type of response from colleges and universities might be a measure of their degree of concern with the lack of an age-related termination-of-employment date for faculty. An important variable in the decision-making process is the significantly larger proportion of the total faculty who will be 55 years of age and older beginning in 1994. This fact alone should cause institutions to recognize the need to take action on other personnel policies—faculty evaluation relating to continued employment, the structure of retirement benefit programs, health insurance coverage, and personnel management activities designed to enhance flexibility of staffing.

REFERENCES

The Educational Resources Information Center (ERIC) Clearing-house on Higher Education abstracts and indexes the current literature on higher education for inclusion in ERIC's database and announcement in ERIC's monthly bibliographic journal, *Resources in Education* (RIE). Most of these publications are available through the ERIC Document Reproduction Service (EDRS). For publications cited in this bibliography that are available from EDRS, ordering number and price are included. Readers who wish to order a publication should write to the ERIC Document Reproduction Service, 3900 Wheeler Avenue, Alexandria, Virginia 22304. (Phone orders with VISA or MasterCard are taken at 800/227-ERIC or 703/823-0500.) When ordering, please specify the document (ED) number. Documents are available as noted in microfiche (MF) and paper copy (PC). Because prices are subject to change, it is advisable to check the latest issue of *Resources in Education* for current cost based on the number of pages in the publication.

American Association of University Professors. September 1978. "The Impact of Federal Retirement-Age Legislation on Higher Education. A Report of the Special Committee on Age Discrimination and Retirement." *AAUP Bulletin* 64: 181–92.

———. September 1980. "Statement of Principles on Academic Retirement and Insurance Plans." *Academe* 66: 321–23.

———. September/October 1982. "Uncapping the Mandatory Retirement Age." *Academe* 68: 4a–18a.

———. 1 March 1983. "Faculty Agreement 1983–1985: Oakland University and the Oakland University Chapter of the American Association of University Professors." ED 257 396. 103 pp. MF–$1.00; PC–$11.41.

———. 1 September 1984. "Agreement between the Administration of Marymount College of Tarrytown, New York, and the Marymount Chapter of the American Association of University Professors, September 1, 1984–August 31, 1986." ED 257 389. 43 pp. MF–$1.00; PC–$5.44.

American Council on Education. 1984. *1984–85 Fact Book on Higher Education.* New York: Macmillan.

———. 1986. "Focus on Faculty." *Higher Education and National Affairs* 35(9): 5.

Baenen, Leonard B., and Ernest, Robert C. August 1982. "An Argument for Early Retirement Incentive Planning." *Personnel Administrator* 27: 63+.

Bagshaw, Marque. 1985. "Managing Resource Uncertainty through Academic Staffing in Four-Year Colleges and Universities." Paper presented at the annual meeting of the Association for the Study of Higher Education, March 15, Chicago, Illinois. ED 259 621. 38 pp. MF–$1.00; PC–$5.44.

Bertelsen, Katherine H. 1983. "Phased Retirement: A Way to Enhance Quality." Paper presented at the annual meeting of the Southern Regional Council on Educational Administration, October, Knoxville, Tennessee. ED 247 652. 39 pp. MF–$1.00; PC–$5.44.

Blackburn, John O., and Schiffman, Susan. 1980. "Faculty Retirement at the COFHE Institutions: An Analysis of the Impact of Age 70 Mandatory Retirement and Options for Institutional Response." Cambridge, Mass.: Consortium on Financing Higher Education. ED 233 643. 90 pp. MF–$1.00; PC–$9.14.

Bowen, Howard R., and Schuster, Jack H. 1986. *American Professors: A National Resource Imperiled*. New York: Oxford University Press.

Calvin, Allen. 1984. "Age Discrimination on Campus." *AAHE Bulletin* 37(3): 1–7. ED 250 999. 7 pp. MF–$1.00; PC–$3.59.

Carbone, Gilbert J. 1983. "Early Retirement of Washington Community College Employees: A Study of the Statutory Early Retirement Program of May–December 1982." Olympia: Washington State Board for Community College Education. ED 238 494. 8 pp. MF–$1.00; PC–$3.59.

Carnegie Council. 1980. *Three Thousand Futures: The Next Twenty Years for Higher Education*. San Francisco: Jossey-Bass.

Carnegie Foundation for the Advancement of Teaching. 1985. "Tracking the Undergraduate Major." *Change* 17(2): 31–33.

Chronister, Jay L. 1984. *The Graying of the Professoriate*. Occasional Paper No. 9. Pittsburgh: University of Pittsburgh, Institute for Higher Education.

Chronister, Jay L., and Trainer, Aileen. 1985a. "Early, Partial, and Phased Retirement Programs in Public Higher Education: A Report on Institutional Experiences." *Journal of the College and University Personnel Association* 36(4): 27–31.

———. 1985b. "A Case Study of the Development of an Early Retirement Program for University Faculty." *Journal of Education Finance* 11(2): 190–204.

Clevenger, Bonnie M., and Chronister, Jay L. 1986. *Early Retirement Programs for Faculty: Three Institutional Case Studies*. Occasional Paper No. 11. Charlottesville: University of Virginia, Center for the Study of Higher Education.

Cliff, Rosemary. March 1974. "Faculty Retirement: A Preliminary Study." Report No. OIS/74-02. Los Angeles: University of Southern California. ED 134 124. 16 pp. MF–$1.00; PC–$3.59.

Commission on College Retirement. May 1986. *A Pension Program for College and University Personnel.* New York: Author.

Cook, Thomas J. 1981. "College Benefit Plans and the Age Discrimination in Employment Act Amendments." *Academe* 67(5): 308–12.

Corwin, Thomas M., and Gross, Anne C. 1979. *Higher Education Responds to Changing Retirement Laws: A Follow-up Report.* Washington, D.C.: American Council on Education, Policy Analysis Service. ED 171 202. 7 pp. MF–$1.00; PC–$3.59.

Corwin, Thomas M., and Knepper, Paula R. 1978. *Finance and Employment Implications of Raising the Mandatory Retirement Age for Faculty.* Washington, D.C.: American Council on Education, Policy Analysis Service. ED 163 868. 72 pp. MF–$1.00; PC–$7.29.

Covert-McGrath, Debra. 1984a. "NACUBO Report: Early and Phased Retirement." *Business Officer* 17(12): 13–16.

———. 1984b. "NACUBO Report: Retirement." *Business Officer* 17(11): 15–16.

Cox, Carole, and Russell, Bonney. 1982. "Preretirement Training: Expanding the Role of the University." Paper presented at the annual meeting of the Gerontological Society of America, November, Boston, Massachusetts. ED 225 465. 14 pp. MF–$1.00; PC–$3.59.

Davis, Bertram H. 1979. "Report of Committee A, 1978–79." *Academe* 65(5): 280–92.

Dorfman, Lorraine T., and others. 1984. "Reactions of Professors to Retirement: A Comparison of Retired Faculty from Three Types of Institutions." *Research in Higher Education* 20(1): 89–102.

Dorfman, Nancy S. 1975. "Inflation's Impact on Faculty Retirement Annuities." *Industrial Gerontology* 2(3): 201–8.

El-Khawas, Elaine. February 1986. *Campus Trends, 1985.* Higher Education Panel Reports No. 71. Washington, D.C.: American Council on Education. ED 267 682. 18 pp. MF–$1.00; PC–$3.59.

Erdmann, Joan E. 1986. "Laws Governing the Involuntary Retirement of Tenured College and University Faculty by Reason of Age." In *Retirement Ages for College and University Personnel.* New York: Commission on College Retirement.

Ernst & Whinney. September 1986. *Tax Reform–1986.* Washington, D.C.: Author.

Felicetti, Daniel A. 1982. "Retirement Options to Offer College Faculty." *Educational Record* 63(3): 22–26.

Fernandez, Luis. 1978. *U.S. Faculty after the Boom: Demographic Projections to the Year 2000.* A Report for the Carnegie Council on Policy Studies in Higher Education. Project on Qualitative Policy Analysis Models of Demand and Supply in Higher Education. Technical Report No. 4. ED 165 618. 192 pp. MF–$1.00; PC–$16.96.

Gross, Alan. 1977a. "Too Old to Teach?" *AGB Reports* 19(5): 28–33.

———. 1977b. "Twilight in Academe: The Problem of the Aging Professoriate." *Phi Delta Kappan* 58(10): 752–55.

Harcleroad, Fred F. 1981. "Escape Routes: Do They Exist?" In *Coping with Faculty Reduction,* edited by Stephen R. Hample. New Directions for Institutional Research No. 30. San Francisco: Jossey-Bass.

Heller, Scott. 1 August 1984. "Adelphi U. Finds 'Fair and Humane Way' to Persuade Professors to Retire Early." *Chronicle of Higher Education* 28: 17 + .

Heller, William F. 1979. "Considerations in Establishing Early Retirement Incentives." Paper presented at the annual meeting of the National Association of College and University Business Attorneys, June 29.

Hopkins, David S. P. 1972. *An Early Retirement Program for the Stanford Faculty: Report and Recommendations.* Palo Alto, Cal.: Stanford University, Academic Planning Office. ED 083 947. 72 pp. MF–$1.00; PC–$7.29.

Hopkins, David S. P., and Massy, William F. 1981. *Planning Models for Colleges and Universities.* Stanford, Cal.: Stanford University Press.

Hughes, Geoffrey C. 1981. "Age 70 Retirement for Faculty: An Institutional Approach." *Research in Higher Education* 15(3): 213–30.

Ingalls, Zoe. 9 January 1985. "Early-Retirement Option in New York State Attracts Hundreds of College Employees." *Chronicle of Higher Education* 30: 27.

Jacobson, Robert L. 23 October 1985. "Nearly 40 Pct. of Faculty Members Said to Consider Leaving Academe." *Chronicle of Higher Education* 31: 1.

Jenny, Hans H. 1974. *Early Retirement: A New Issue in Higher Education. The Financial Consequences of Early Retirement.* New York: TIAA/CREF.

———. 1981. "Can Anyone Afford to Retire in an Age of Inflation?" Paper presented at the annual forum of the Association for Institutional Research, May, Minneapolis, Minnesota. ED 205 091. 41 pp. MF–$1.00; PC–$7.29.

Jenny, Hans H.; Heim, Peggy; and Hughes, Geoffrey C. 1979. *Another Challenge: Age 70 Retirement in Higher Education.* New York: TIAA/CREF. ED 177 940. 86 pp. MF–$1.00; PC–$9.14.

Johnstone, William A. 1980. "Faculty Retrenchment in the 1980s: A Question of How Many? And How Managed?" *Journal of the College and University Personnel Association* 31(1): 22–30.

Kell, Diane, and Patton, Carl V. 1978. "Reaction to Induced Early Retirement." *Gerontologist* 18(2): 173–78.

Kepple, Thomas R., Jr. 1984. "Incentive Faculty Early Retirement Programs at Independent Liberal Arts Colleges." Doctoral dissertation, Syracuse University.

King, Francis P. 1983. "Faculty Retirement: Early, Normal, and Late." In *Issues in Faculty Personnel Policies,* edited by Jon W. Fuller. New Directions for Higher Education No. 41. San Francisco: Jossey-Bass.

King, Francis P., and Cook, Thomas J. 1980. *Benefit Plans in Higher Education.* New York: Columbia University Press.

King, Judith D., and others. 28 February 1977. *The Faculty Salary and Budget Committee Report on Early Retirement (Grand Valley State Colleges, Michigan).* ED 138 143. 13 pp. MF–$1.00; PC–$3.59.

Kreinin, Mordechai E. 1982. "Preserving Tenure Commitments in Hard Times." *Academe* 68(2): 37–45.

Licata, Christine M. 1986. *Post-tenure Faculty Evaluation: Threat or Opportunity?* ASHE-ERIC Higher Education Report No. 1. Washington, D.C.: Association for the Study of Higher Education. ED 270 009. 110 pp. MF–$1.00; PC–$11.41.

Mitchell, Barbara A. 1981. "Early Retirement in Higher Education." Paper presented at the annual meeting of the Association for the Study of Higher Education, March 3, Washington, D.C. ED 203 802. 16 pp. MF–$1.00; PC–$3.59.

Mortimer, Kenneth P.; Bagshaw, Marque; and Caruso, Annette. 1985. *Academic Reallocation: A National Profile.* University Park, Pa.: Pennsylvania State University, Center for the Study of Higher Education.

Mortimer, Kenneth P.; Bagshaw, Marque; and Masland, Andrew T. 1985. *Flexibility in Academic Staffing: Effective Policies and Practices.* ASHE-ERIC Higher Education Report No. 1. Washington, D.C.: Association for the Study of Higher Education. ED 260 675. 121 pp. MF–$1.00; PC–$10.99.

Mulanaphy, James M. 1981. *Plans and Expectations for Retirement of TIAA/CREF Participants.* New York: Teachers Insurance and Annuity Association. ED 208 785. 78 pp. MF–$1.00; PC–$9.14.

National Association of College and University Business Officers. 1986a. "Employers Must Continue Retirement Contributions for Older Workers." *Business Officer* 20(6): 9.

———. 1986b. "Retirement Starts Earlier, Lasts Longer." *Business Officer* 20(3): 13–14.

———. 1986c. "Tax Reform Legislation Is Approved by Congress." *Business Officer* 20(4): 10+.

National Center for Education Statistics. 1979. *Digest of Education Statistics, 1979*. Washington, D.C.: U.S. Government Printing Office. ED 172 458. 255 pp. MF–$1.00; PC–$19.64.

Nevison, Christopher H. 1980. "Effects of Tenure and Retirement Policies on the College Faculty: A Case Study Using Computer Simulation." *Journal of Higher Education* 51(2): 150–66.

Novotny, Janet. 1981. *Mandatory Retirement of Higher Education Faculty*. AAHE-ERIC Higher Education Research Currents. Washington, D.C.: American Association for Higher Education. ED 197 693. 6 pp. MF–$1.00; PC–$3.59.

Oi, Walter Y. 1979. "Academic Tenure and Mandatory Retirement under the New Law." *Science* 206(4425): 1373–78.

Palmer, D. D., and Patton, Carl V. 1978. "Attitudes toward Incentive Early Retirement Schemes." In *Current Issues in Higher Education: Changing Retirement Policies*. Washington, D.C.: American Association for Higher Education.

Palmer, Stacey E. 1 February 1984. "Early Retirement: For Some Teachers, Financial Incentives Seem Inadequate." *Chronicle of Higher Education* 27: 23–24.

Patton, Carl V. 1977. "Early Retirement in Academia: Making the Decision." *Gerontologist* 17(4): 347–53.

———. 1978. "Mid-Career Change and Early Retirement." In *Evaluating Faculty Performance and Vitality,* edited by Wayne Kirschling. New Directions for Institutional Research No. 20. San Francisco: Jossey-Bass.

———. 1979. *Academia in Transition: Mid-Career Change or Early Retirement*. Cambridge, Mass.: Abt Books.

———. 7 February 1983a. "Incentives and Career Change Options—A Personal and Legal Perspective." A tape of a teleconference sponsored by the American Council on Education.

———. 1983b. "Institutional Practices and Faculty Who Leave." In *College Faculty: Versatile Human Resources in a Period of Constraint,* edited by Roger G. Baldwin and Robert T. Blackburn. New Directions for Institutional Research No. 40. San Francisco: Jossey-Bass.

———. 1983c. "Voluntary Alternatives to Forced Termination." *Academe* 69(1): 1a–8a.

Peat, Marwick, Mitchell & Company. 21 August 1986. *Tax Reform Act of 1986: Conference Agreement*. Washington, D.C.: Author.

Price Waterhouse. October 1986. *The Price Waterhouse Guide to the New Tax Law*. New York: Bantam Books.

Public Law 95-2256. 6 April 1978. Age Discrimination in Employment Act Amendments of 1978.

Public Law 99-509. 17 October 1986. Omnibus Budget Reconciliation Act of 1986.

Public Law 99-514. 22 October 1986. Tax Reform Act of 1986.

Public Law 99-592. 31 October 1986. Age Discrimination in Employment Act Amendments of 1986.

Radner, Roy, and Kuh, Charlotte V. 1978. *Preserving a Lost Generation: Policies to Assure a Steady Flow of Young Scholars until the Year 2000. A Report and Recommendations, October 1978.* Berkeley, Cal.: Carnegie Commission on Higher Education. ED 165 575. 63 pp. MF–$1.00; PC–$7.29.

Reinhard, Raymond M. August 1981. *An Analysis of the California State University and Colleges Early Retirement Incentive Program: A Report Pursuant to Chapter 656 of the Statutes of 1979.* Sacramento: California State Legislative Analyst's Office. ED 215 606. 124 pp. MF–$1.00; PC–$10.99.

Ruebhausen, Oscar M. 1986. "Age as a Criterion for the Retirement of Tenured Faculty." In *Retirement Ages for College and University Personnel.* New York: Commission on College Retirement.

Schuster, Jack H., and Bowen, Howard R. 1985. "The Faculty at Risk." *Change* 17(5): 12–21.

Shapiro, Larry E. 1980. "Early Retirement from Colleges and Universities: Considerations under the Employee Retirement Income Security Act." *Journal of College and University Law* 7(1): 174–79.

Simpson, William A. 1979. "Steady State Effects of a Later Mandatory Retirement Law for Tenured Faculty." *Research in Higher Education* 11(1): 37–44.

Soldofsky, Robert M. Spring 1981. "A Plan to Encourage Early Retirement." *Journal of the College and University Personnel Association* 32: 33–36.

Spreadbury, Connie. 1984. "Innovative Plans to Encourage Senior Faculty to Take Early Retirement." *Journal of the National Association of Women Deans, Administrators, and Counselors* 47(3): 14–20.

Taylor, Alton L., and Coolidge, Herbert E. 1974. "Survey and Analysis of Early Retirement Policies." *Educational Record* 55(3): 183–87.

Teachers Insurance and Annuity Association. 1986. *Planning for Health Coverage in Retirement—Medicare and Health Insurance.* New York: TIAA, Educational Research Unit.

Tillinghast, Nelson, and Warren, Inc. December 1979. *Potential Financial and Employment Impact of Age 70 Mandatory*

Retirement Legislation on COFHE Institutions. Cambridge, Mass.: Consortium on Financing Higher Education. ED 233 644. 79 pp. MF–$1.00; PC–$9.14.

Toevs, Alden L., and Handhardt, Arthur, Jr. Fall 1982. "The Effect of Early Retirement Incentives on Faculty Quality." *The Collegiate Forum:* 6.

Turnbull, Augustus B., III. 1986. "The Various Early Retirement Programs of the Florida State University." Mimeographed. Tallahassee: Florida State University.

Walker, George H., Jr. 1972. "Status of Phased Retirement in Higher Education." Mount Pleasant, Mich.: Central Michigan University. ED 054 752. 8 pp. MF–$1.00; PC–$3.59.

Watkins, Beverly T. 10 July 1985. "Early-Retirement Options Gaining Popularity among Colleges and Older Faculty Members." *Chronicle of Higher Education* 30: 19 + .

———. 30 July 1986. "House Panel Votes to End Forced Retirement for College Employees." *Chronicle of Higher Education* 32(22): 23 + .

Weiler, William C. 1981. "Simulation of Institutional Incentive Plans for Faculty Early Retirement Using a Behavioral Model of Retirement Decision Making." *Research in Higher Education* 15(2): 129–39.

West, David A. 28 October 1980. "Faculty Morale and Career Choice in the 1980s." Mimeographed. Columbia: University of Missouri. ED 192 703. 6 pp. MF–$1.00; PC–$3.59.

White, Gloria W. Summer 1981. "Bridge over Troubled Waters: An Approach to Early Retirement." *Journal of the College and University Personnel Association* 32: 8–12.

INDEX

A

AAUP (see American Association for University Professors)
Actuarial projection, 13, 40
Ad hoc faculty committees, 26, 27
Ad hoc plans, 11
Adelphi University: incentive options, 52
Age (see also Mandatory retirement age)
      choice of for retirement, 38, 60
      health insurance implications, 19
      length of service, 18
      median, 4
      "normal" retirement, 16
      projection, 36
      sample graphs, 29
      targeted groups, 33
Age Discrimination in Employment Act (ADEA), 3, 4, 6, 8, 11,
   16, 21, 58, 61, 65
American Association for University Professors (AAUP), 41, 49
Annuities
      enhancements, 13–14
      premium continuation, 13, 31
      retirement plans, 17–18
      supplemental plans, 22
      tax-sheltered, 22

B

Baseline effectiveness, 50
Boards of trustees, 27
Bridging payments, 14, 20, 39, 40, 43, 47, 50
Buyout incentive, 52

C

California Public Employees' Retirement System, 48
California State Teacher's Retirement System, 48
California state university and colleges: service credit, 18, 48, 51
City University of New York: service credit, 48
Colgate University: computer simulation model, 35
Collective bargaining agreements
      effective dates, 22
      eligibility, 57
      reemployment, 49
College Retirement Equity Fund (see TIAA-CREF)
Community college personnel, 55
Compensation
      package, 15
      savings, 55

Computer simulations, 36
Contracts
    for early retirement, 32
    tenured faculty, 52
Cost/benefit analysis
    considerations, 37, 55, 64
    faculty perspective, 38–41
    generic formula, 42–45
    institutional perspective, 41–42
Costs
    age/tenure status implication, 6
    consideration, 37
    generic formula, 42–45
    projection, 12
Curriculum trends, 6–7

D
Deferred compensation, 16, 22
Deferred early retirement, 53
Deferred payments, 13
Defined contribution/benefit plans, 17, 18, 22, 40
Departmental priorities, 32, 58–59
Dependent insurance, 20
Deterrents, 56–57

E
Effectiveness
    faculty perspective, 56–57
    institutional perspective, 50–56
Eligibility for participation, 57–58, 60–61
Employee Retirement Income Security Act of 1974 (ERISA), 21, 22
Employment Retirement Income Security Act, 45

F
Faculty
    age, 29
    growth of full-time, 3
    loss of distinguished, 57
    retirement pace, 28–30
    role in program establishment, 25–27
    satisfaction, 56
    senate, 26
    support, 51, 52
    targeted, 30–32
    tenure status, 5–6

P
Part-time employment, 14, 32, 39, 49, 54, 60
Partial retirement plans, 14–15, 61
Participation limits, 33
Payment options, 12–15, 59
Pennsylvania State University: Markov model use, 35
Perquisites, 15
Phased employment, 49
Phased retirement, 14–15, 47–48, 53, 61
Planning models, 34–37
Preretirement
 counseling, 64
 supplemental plan, 50
Presidential involvement, 25
Program administration, 64
Program structures, 11–12
Project on Reallocation, 47
Public Law 99–509, 22
Public Law 99–514, 22
Public Law 99–592, 5, 11

R
Reemployment, 49, 54, 60
Resource management, 50
Retirement income (see Income)
Retirement preparation programs, 64
Rhodes College
 dual option program, 53
 planned objective, 27

S
Salary
 continuation, 16
 level, 6
 reduction, 49
Self-esteem, 41
Service credit, 18, 48, 51, 52, 55
Severance pay, 12–13, 47, 52, 53
Social security, 14, 32, 39, 40
Spouses, 20
Staffing flexibility, 5, 6, 26
Standard of living, 65
Stanford University
 Markov model use, 35
 targeted faculty, 31
State legislation, 54, 63

ASHE-ERIC HIGHER EDUCATION REPORTS

Since 1983, the Association for the Study of Higher Education (ASHE) and the ERIC Clearinghouse on Higher Education at The George Washington University have cosponsored the ASHE-ERIC Higher Education Report series. The 1987 series is the sixteenth series overall, with the American Association for Higher Education having served as cosponsor before 1983.

Each monograph is the definitive analysis of a tough higher education problem, based on a thorough research of pertinent literature and institutional experiences. After topics are identified by a national survey, noted practitioners and scholars write the reports, with experts reviewing each manuscript before publication.

Eight monographs (10 monographs before 1985) in the ASHE-ERIC Higher Education Report series are published each year, available individually or by subscription. Subscription to eight issues is $60 regular; $50 for members of AERA, AAHE, and AIR; $40 for members of ASHE. (Add $7.50 for postage outside the United States.)

Prices for single copies, including 4th class postage and handling, are $10.00 regular and $7.50 for members of AERA, AAHE, AIR, and ASHE ($7.50 regular and $6.00 for members for 1983 and 1984 reports, $6.50 regular and $5.00 for members for reports published before 1983). If faster 1st class postage is desired for U.S. and Canadian orders, add $.75 for each publication ordered; overseas, add $4.50. For VISA and MasterCard payments, include card number, expiration date, and signature. Orders under $25 must be prepaid. Bulk discounts are available on orders of 15 or more reports (not applicable to subscriptions). Order from the Publications Department, Association for the Study of Higher Education, One Dupont Circle, Suite 630, Washington, D.C. 20036-1183, 202/296-2597. Write for a publication list of all the Higher Education Reports available.

1987 ASHE-ERIC Higher Education Reports

1. Incentive Early Retirement Programs for Faculty: Innovative Responses to a Changing Environment
   Jay L. Chronister and Thomas R. Kepple, Jr.

1986 ASHE-ERIC Higher Education Reports

1. Post-tenure Faculty Evaluation: Threat or Opportunity?
   Christine M. Licata

2. Blue Ribbon Commissions and Higher Education: Changing Academe from the Outside
   Janet R. Johnson and Laurence R. Marcus

3. Responsive Professional Education: Balancing Outcomes and Opportunities
   Joan S. Stark, Malcolm A. Lowther, and Bonnie M.K. Hagerty

4. Increasing Students' Learning: A Faculty Guide to Reducing Stress among Students
   Neal A. Whitman, David C. Spendlove, and Claire H. Clark

5. Student Financial Aid and Women: Equity Dilemma?
   Mary Moran

6. The Master's Degree: Tradition, Diversity, Innovation
   Judith S. Glazer

7. The College, the Constitution, and the Consumer Student: Implications for Policy and Practice
   Robert M. Hendrickson and Annette Gibbs

8. Selecting College and University Personnel: The Quest and the Questions
   Richard A. Kaplowitz

1985 ASHE-ERIC Higher Education Reports

1. Flexibility in Academic Staffing: Effective Policies and Practices
   Kenneth P. Mortimer, Marque Bagshaw, and Andrew T. Masland

2. Associations in Action: The Washington, D.C., Higher Education Community
   Harland G. Bloland

3. And on the Seventh Day: Faculty Consulting and Supplemental Income
   Carol M. Boyer and Darrell R. Lewis

4. Faculty Research Performance: Lessons from the Sciences and Social Sciences
   John W. Creswell

5. Academic Program Reviews: Institutional Approaches, Expectations, and Controversies
   Clifton F. Conrad and Richard F. Wilson

6. Students in Urban Settings: Achieving the Baccalaureate Degree
   Richard C. Richardson, Jr., and Louis W. Bender

7. Serving More Than Students: A Critical Need for College Student Personnel Services
   Peter H. Garland

8. Faculty Participation in Decision Making: Necessity or Luxury?
   Carol E. Floyd

1984 ASHE-ERIC Higher Education Reports

1. Adult Learning: State Policies and Institutional Practices
   K. Patricia Cross and Anne-Marie McCartan

2. Student Stress: Effects and Solutions
   Neal A. Whitman, David C. Spendlove, and Claire H. Clark

3. Part-time Faculty: Higher Education at a Crossroads
   Judith M. Gappa

4. Sex Discrimination Law in Higher Education: The Lessons of the Past Decade
   J. Ralph Lindgren, Patti T. Ota, Perry A. Zirkel, and Nan Van Gieson

5. Faculty Freedoms and Institutional Accountability: Interactions and Conflicts
   Steven G. Olswang and Barbara A. Lee

6. The High-Technology Connection: Academic/Industrial Cooperation for Economic Growth
   Lynn G. Johnson

82

7. Employee Educational Programs: Implications for Industry and
Higher Education
   Suzanne W. Morse

8. Academic Libraries: The Changing Knowledge Centers of Colleges
and Universities
   Barbara B. Moran

9. Futures Research and the Strategic Planning Process: Implications for
Higher Education
   James L. Morrison, William L. Renfro, and Wayne I. Boucher

10. Faculty Workload: Research, Theory, and Interpretation
    Harold E. Yuker

1983 ASHE-ERIC Higher Education Reports

1. The Path to Excellence: Quality Assurance in Higher Education
   Laurence R. Marcus, Anita O. Leone, and Edward D. Goldberg

2. Faculty Recruitment, Retention, and Fair Employment: Obligations
and Opportunities
   John S. Waggaman

3. Meeting the Challenges: Developing Faculty Careers
   Michael C. T. Brookes and Katherine L. German

4. Raising Academic Standards: A Guide to Learning Improvement
   Ruth Talbott Keimig

5. Serving Learners at a Distance: A Guide to Program Practices
   Charles E. Feasley

6. Competence, Admissions, and Articulation: Returning to the Basics
in Higher Education
   Jean L. Preer

7. Public Service in Higher Education: Practices and Priorities
   Patricia H. Crosson

8. Academic Employment and Retrenchment: Judicial Review and
Administrative Action
   Robert M. Hendrickson and Barbara A. Lee

9. Burnout: The New Academic Disease
   Winifred Albizu Meléndez and Rafael M. de Guzmán

10. Academic Workplace: New Demands, Heightened Tensions
    Ann E. Austin and Zelda F. Gamson